I0123543

I dedicate this to my parents, Jill Carter (Cave) and Richard Hood Ward, and to my brother, Carter.

My sincere thanks to Antonio Oppi for his indispensable advice and help in finding a publisher; to Lorie Szarek, at Clearfield Company, for her many excellent suggestions; to the kind and helpful Virginia ladies, Julie Bushong at the Culpeper Genealogical Society and Marianne Hurd at the Orange County Historical Society; and, of course, to Stathe and Melissa for their support.

CONTENTS

ABBREVIATIONS

OCDB (1–8)   John Frederick Dorman, comp. *Orange County, Virginia: Deed Books 1–8, 1735–1743*. Vols. 3 in 1. Washington, D.C., 1961–1971.

OCDB (9–20)   Ruth and Sam Sparacio, comps. *Deed Abstracts of Orange County, Virginia, 1743–1779 (Deed Books 9–20)*. 5 vols. McLean, Va., 1985–88.

OCWB   John Frederick Dorman, comp. *Orange County, Virginia, Will Books 1–2: 1735–1778*. Vols. 2 in 1. Washington, D.C., 1958–1961.

SCDB (A)   Lydia Sparacio Bontempo, comp. *Deed Book Abstracts of Spotsylvania County, Virginia, 1728 to 1729*. Springfield, Va., ca. 2002.

SCDB (B)   Lydia Sparacio Bontempo, comp. *Deed Book Abstracts of Spotsylvania County, Virginia, 1730 to 1731*. Springfield, Va., ca. 2004.

StGVB   John Frederick Dorman, transc. and ed. *Saint George's Parish, Spotsylvania County, Virginia: Vestry Books, 1726–1817*. Fredericksburg, Va., 1998.

StMVB   Rosalie Edith Davis, transcr. and ed. *Saint Mark Parish Vestry Book and Levies 1730–1785: Spotsylvania, Orange and Culpeper Counties, Virginia*. Manchester, Mo., 1983.

VPB   State of Virginia. "Virginia Land Office Patents and Grants." Database and images. *Library of Virginia*.

THE COLONIAL CHURCHES OF ST. THOMAS' PARISH, ORANGE COUNTY, VIRGINIA

With Notes on Sites in Orange, Greene, and Madison Counties

By
Lizabeth Ward Papageorgiou

CLEARFIELD

Printed for
Clearfield Company by
Genealogical Publishing Co.
Baltimore, Maryland
2008

ISBN-13: 978-0-8063-5377-7
ISBN-10: 0-8063-5377-5

Made in the United States of America

PREFACE

An examination of the colonial churches in St. Thomas' Parish, Orange County, Virginia, is long overdue. Although important contributions have been made to bits and pieces of this subject since the first, chiefly anecdotal history by Rev. Joseph Earnest in Bishop William Meade's *Old Churches, Ministers, and Families of Virginia* in 1857,[1] it is now possible to examine the subject afresh relying solely on eighteenth-century parish vestry books, county court orders and road orders, patents, deeds, wills and newspapers.

The primary documents used in this study are the county court road orders in Nathaniel Mason Pawlett's *Spotsylvania County Road Orders 1722–1734* and Ann Brush Miller's *Orange County Road Orders 1734–1749* and *Orange County Road Orders 1750–1800*.[2] Because footnoting each reference to a road order would be cumbersome, road orders, which specifically refer to a chapel or church, appear in the text in bold (**2 June 1731**) and are quoted in full in **Appendix I**. Road orders of the same date are differentiated by a superscript letter (**2 June 1731[A], 2 June 1731[B]**). All other road orders appear in regular type followed by a page number (2 July 1732 p. 3). The page following the date is from the published transcriptions, not the original document. Other documents cited in an abbreviated form in the text—for example, *Saint Mark Parish Vestry Book and Levies 1730–1785* (*StMVB*)—are found in the **Abbreviations**. All quotes from these and other eighteenth-century documents retain their original and often peculiar punctuation and orthography.

Up until 1752, all Virginia documents used the "Old Style" dating of the Julian calendar with the beginning of the year on 25 March; thus, 1 January to 24 March 1732 (O.S.) was 1733. From 1752, the "New Style" dating of the Gregorian calendar was adopted. In this work, pre-1752 documents dated 1 January to 24 March note both the Old and New Style date (2 February 1732/33).

When referring to Culpeper, Madison or Greene Counties before their formation in 1749, 1793 and 1838, respectively, the counties are in quotations; i.e., In 1732, William Lucas patented land on Swift Run in "Greene" County.

Unfortunately, there is no map of colonial St. Thomas' Parish, which encompasses today's Orange, Greene and southern Madison Counties and combines contemporary roadways and detailed geographical features—something on the order of Eugene M. Scheel's map of Madison County. In lieu of such a map, the following can be used: *Topozone.com*, a website with United States Geological Survey maps; the map of Orange County in Ann Miller's *Antebellum Orange: The Pre-Civil War Homes, Public Buildings and Historic Sites of Orange County, Virginia*; and Scheel's map of Madison County.[3]

INTRODUCTION

The Anglican Church in Virginia

Unlike New England, which had been settled by Puritans and Congregationalists, Virginia, as set out in the charter granted to the Virginia Company by King James I in 1606, was to adhere to the faith of the mother country, and the local government was to ensure the operation of the Anglican church throughout the colony. Other churches were allowed restricted rights to operate in Virginia under the Act of Toleration of 1689 (adopted 1699 in Virginia) so long as they did not threaten the predominance and authority of the Anglican church.

Counties were the administrative divisions of Virginia and parishes the Anglican church's divisions; in most cases, parish and county shared the same borders. When warranted by the growth and spread of settlements within a parish, a new parish was formed and a few years later the boundaries of the new parish usually became a new county. As soon as a new parish was formed, all free white males—"free holders and house keepers of the said Parish"—were ordered to meet to "Elect and Choose twelve of the most able and Discreet persons of their Parish to be vestry Men" (*StMVB*, 7). Only the most prominent men of the county were elected to the vestry and upon election were automatically entitled the appellation "gentleman." It was understood that election to the vestry was a stepping stone to political power and appointment as county justice, sheriff, officer of the militia and election to the House of Burgesses. (When Orange County was formed in 1734, one-third of the new county's vestrymen were appointed justices, one became sheriff and one was elected a burgess.) After the election of the first vestry, democracy ended and all replacements for this life-term office were chosen by the vestry itself—usually a relative of the departed vestryman.

Although the vestry books—minutes of the vestry meetings and parish accounts—of St. Thomas' Parish have not survived, those of St. Mark's and St. George's Parishes are almost completely intact and reveal a great deal about the workings of a parish vestry. The St. Mark's vestry held their meetings as need required at the vestry house, one of the churches or chapels, or at the glebe, the residence of the parish minister. In their first busy year, the St. Mark's vestry met seven times; then, from 1732 to 1740, they met an average of three times a year. Apparently vestrymen were not required to attend each meeting: Benjamin Cave and James Barbour, who lived in what would become St. Thomas' Parish, attended less than a third of the meetings between 1731 and 1740.

The vestry, not the parish minister, managed the parish. They hired—on the recommendation of the governor—and could discipline and dismiss the parish minister. Only ministers ordained in England were permitted to preach in Virginia and the rigors of life in the new colony did not encourage applicants; well-qualified ministers were scarce, and many who took up positions in Virginia were scallywags and adventurers. When no permanent minister could be found, the vestry hired supply ministers to preach by the sermon and paid laymen to read the service at distant chapels and churches. The vestry chose the location of new churches, chapels and the glebe and hired and paid workers to build and maintain them. They recorded baptisms, marriages and funerals (no such records survive from St. Mark's or St. Thomas' Parishes). They provided aide to sick and poor parishioners and took responsibility for orphaned, neglected or illegitimate children. Two church wardens, members of the vestry, were appointed annually to implement decisions of the vestry, such as collecting the parish levy, buying parish properties, as well as fining parishioners for drunkenness, blasphemy and not attending church.[1] Once a year, the vestry met to prepare a budget to cover salaries of the minister, clerk, sextons and readers; construction and maintenance of parish buildings; and assistance to the needy. They then divided the number of tithables in the parish—all men aged sixteen and older and all non-white women aged sixteen and older and engaged in tobacco production—into the future budget to determine how much each tithable was to be taxed.

Each parish had a principal parish church and, scattered throughout the parish, other churches and small, probably crude "chapels of ease," which were usually served by readers. (Only Anglican houses of worship could be called a church or chapel; other denominations met at meetinghouses.)[2] Regular church attendance, required by law of everyone twenty-one years or older, was not only for the sake of the soul but was also a welcome social occasion for parishioners to witness baptisms and marriages and hear announcements of new laws, local news, marriage banns and gossip (see **18 March 1734/35[A]**, **18 November 1735[B]**). In 1731, only the parish church at Germanna; the Fork Chapel, about four miles northwest of Germanna; and the Southwest Mountain Chapel, many miles southwest of Germanna, served the parishioners of the enormous, newly formed parish of St. Mark. Many parishioners lived too far away to attend services regularly (coach travel was rare and most households did not have enough horses for everyone), and even families living only a few miles from a church or chapel needed several hours to plod the rough roads to Sunday services.

Roads in Colonial Virginia

Invaluable evidence for the histories and locations of the churches and chapels in St. Thomas' Parish can be found in the orders to construct and maintain roads recorded in the county court order books. As Ann Brush Miller pointed out in the introduction to *Orange County Road Orders 1734–1749*, "Most of this early road network still remains in place and in service." In other words, many of the colonial roads described in these road orders can be identified with contemporary roads in greater Orange County.[1] Many of these road orders challenge understanding: the names of topographical features changed over the years, some runs or sites no longer exist and the court often referred to a "Church" or "Chapel" without specifying which church or chapel. Because the road orders are the backbone of this work, a brief description of the colonial Virginia road system will be helpful.

European scouts and explorers who ventured into the Rapidan

River region in the seventeenth century usually followed Indian trails, many of which were age-old animal paths. But when families settled in the region in the early eighteenth century, it was necessary to widen these old paths and clear new roads for foot travel, horseback and pack-trains (carriages did not become common until around 1762).[2] This need for roads can be seen in the number of roads ordered constructed during the first sessions of the Spotsylvania County court in 1722.

Virginia adopted the English system of obliging each county to build and maintain its roads. From the early seventeenth century, the Virginia Assembly passed many laws setting out specific requirements for roads; for instance, a 1748 law ordered the construction and maintenance of roads "passing to, and from . . . the court house . . . the parish churches, and all public mills, and ferries."[3] In addition to these public roads, people could petition the court for roads in their neighborhood. After a petition was made, the court appointed men to find the best route for the petitioned road. If the court approved the proposal presented to them, the clearing of the proposed road was assigned to an overseer and a working force of tithables living in the neighborhood of the proposed road. Each tithable was legally obliged to do road work six to eight days a year and to supply the tools, wagons and draft animals needed.

After a new road was cleared, the court assigned an overseer and a work force to maintain the road and any bridges along the road. These assignments could last from a few months to several years. In the early eighteenth century, a road assigned to an overseer was often very long; for example, in 1722, a road over forty-five miles long from the Southwest Mountains to the Wilderness Bridge was assigned to one overseer (7 August 1722 p. 5). But as the number of settlers grew, the roads were divided into smaller sections and assigned to more overseers. Maintenance of the roads was crucial for the county; even during the years of the Revolutionary War, roadwork continued. Overseers who did not clear or maintain their roads, or did poor work or did not set up direction signs at crossroads with "Inscriptions thereon in large letters directing to the most noted place to which each of the said Joyning roads leads" were fined by the court.[4] The Orange County court order books are filled with such complaints and fines against overseers for dereliction of their duties.

The most important roads in the county were "rowling [rolling] roads" for transporting tobacco—the crop of currency in Virginia—to the commercial centers. Although it was easier to transport tobacco by river or runs, the waterways were not convenient to everyone and not always passable. Tobacco was transported by "hogsheads," a large, five-foot long, tobacco-filled barrel through the center of which passed a rope, which was harnessed to draft animals and rolled. Continuous passage of these large and heavy hogsheads widened these rolling roads and made them major arteries for wagon travel.

But no matter how well maintained, these roads were no more than dirt-packed paths. Most were narrow, tree-blazed tracks only wide enough for horse or foot traffic; the wider rolling roads were deeply rutted from the heavy hogsheads, and both were muddy in the rainy season and dusty in the dry. Travel was slow, especially in the heavily watered county of Orange. Streams and rivers were crossed at fords, or over bridges, or across the tops of milldams (mill owners were required to build and maintain wagon ways over their mills) or by ferry. Bridges, because of their rough-hewn construction, were often worse than fords; it was not unusual for travelers to have to repair washed out sections of a bridge before continuing on their way.

St. George's Parish: Grandparent of St. Thomas' Parish, 1721–1731

In 1714, Alexander Spotswood, lieutenant governor of the Virginia colony, constructed a fortress in the unsettled northern wilderness near the Rapidan River to house forty-two Germans, whom he had hired and transported to the area to work his mines. Spotswood called the settlement, with its crude houses and a "blockhouse" where these German Reformed Protestants worshiped, Germanna. This blockhouse was the first house of worship within the borders of what would become St. Thomas' Parish. Because Germanna was so far from other settlements, and the German Protestants did not speak English, the Virginia Assembly granted them, for seven years, their own parish, which extended in a five-mile radius around Germanna. Within this parish, called St. George, the Germans could hold their own services, hire a minister and were exempt from taxes to the Anglican church. The Germans remained in the Germanna area until 1725 or 1726.[1]

Seven years after the fortress at Germanna was built, in May of 1721, Spotsylvania County was formed from King and Queen, Essex, and King William Counties. It encompassed all of today's Spotsylvania, Orange, Culpeper, Madison, Greene and Rappahannock Counties and the counties west of the Blue Ridge Mountains. The new parish of St. George—an enlarged version of the German Protestant parish—served this enormous, albeit sparsely populated, county.

Lt. Gov. Spotswood chose Germanna to be the seat of the new county because it was convenient to his vast land holdings. He immediately built a courthouse in Germanna (the court held its first session there in 1722) and began construction of an Anglican church. Businesses soon followed, and the crude fortress was transformed into the political and economic center of the new county. However, the St. George's vestry, reflecting the views of the county's settlers, argued that Germanna was too far from the concentrated settlements in the southeast of the county to be the administrative center of the county, and in 1732 the seat of government was moved to Fredericksburg.

Although Spotswood's church at Germanna was the earliest proposed church, it was not the first church built in St. George's Parish. By 1724, two churches—the Mattapony Church, on the Ta River, and the Rappahannock Church, at the intersection of the Mine and Massaponax roads—had been built on the orders of the St. George's vestry. The Germanna Church was probably in operation by 1726, and some time around 1729 the Fork Chapel and the Southwest Mountain Chapel were added to the parish.[2]

St. Mark's Parish:
Parent of St. Thomas' Parish, 1731–1740

On 21 May 1730, less than a decade after the formation of St. George's Parish, the Virginia Assembly, recognizing the "many inconveniences [which] attend the parishioners of Saint George parish, in the county of Spotsylvania, by reason of the great length thereof," passed an act to form a new parish out of St. George.[1] The parish of St. George was reduced to the boundaries of today's Spotsylvania County, and the new parish of St. Mark encompassed the immense area of today's Orange, Culpeper, Madison, Greene and Rappahannock Counties and the counties west of the Blue Ridge Mountains. On 1 January 1731, the parishioners of St. Mark's Parish met at the Germanna Church and elected their vestrymen. Less than four years later, Orange County, encompassing St. Mark's Parish, was established; and on 21 January 1735, the newly appointed justices of Orange County held the first meeting of the Orange County court.

The Germanna Church, the Fork Chapel and the Southwest Mountain Chapel were within the boundaries of the newly formed St. Mark's Parish. Between 1731 and 1740, when St. Thomas' Parish was formed from St. Mark's, the St. Mark's vestry built five houses of worship: the Great Fork Church, which replaced the burnt Germanna Church and supplanted the Fork Chapel; the Southwest Mountain Church, which replaced the Southwest Mountain Chapel; the Upper Chapel; the North Chapel and the Little Fork Chapel. Even after the formation of St. Thomas' Parish in 1740, roads to the churches, chapels and glebe in St. Mark's Parish remained the responsibility of the Orange County court until 1750 when Culpeper County, which contained St. Mark's Parish, was formed from Orange County. (Roads ordered by the Orange County court to houses of worship in St. Mark's Parish from 1735 to 1749 appear in **Appendix I**).

The Fork Chapel, documented as early as 1729 (*StGVB*, 10), was north of Germanna in the Great Fork of the Rapidan and Rappahannock Rivers near Lignum in "Culpeper" County.[2] It appears to have been abandoned upon completion of the nearby Great Fork Church in 1733, since on 10 October 1732 the St. Mark's vestry ordered William Payton to continue as reader at the Fork Chapel in 1733 until the parish church was finished and then be reader there (*StMVB*, 11), and thereafter no mention of the Fork Chapel appears in the vestry book. (It is peculiar that no road orders to the Fork Chapel can be identified.) This old Fork Chapel is sometimes confused with a later Little Fork Chapel in "Culpeper" County in the Little Fork of the Hazel and Hedgman (Rappahannock) Rivers near Rixeyville, which was first mentioned in the St. Mark's vestry book on 14 October 1740 (*StMVB*, 28).[3] There was also another Fork Chapel, which appears in the road orders between **16 December 1735** and **22 May 1737**.[4] On **16 December 1735**, James Barbour was given permission to clear a road from the "South West Mountain ffork Chappell to Capt: Bellfields Plantation." This cannot be the Southwest Mountain Chapel, which was not located in a fork, was never so described in other documents, and by 1734 had been replaced by the Southwest Mountain Church (see below). That this "South West Mountain ffork Chappell" is a miswriting, is confirmed by a later order on **17 February 1735/36**, which expanded on the **16 December 1735** order but described the road going from the "Chappell in the Little fork to Capt. Bellfields Quarter." Ann L. Miller suggested that these two orders referred to the North Chapel, built in 1735, or the Little Fork German Reformed Chapel, built by the German Reformed Protestants. Both chapels were in a third "Little Fork," the fork of the Rapidan and Robinson Rivers in "Madison" County.[5]

The Great Fork Church, the first church built by the St. Mark's vestry, was near the old Fork Chapel and replaced the Germanna Church, which burned down in 1732. On 13 May and 30 June 1732, the vestry ordered this new parish church to be ready for services by August 1733 and completed by May 1734 at a cost of 36,000 pounds of tobacco. On **6 September 1732[A]**, **8 November 1732** and **7 February 1732/33[A&B]**, roads were ordered to the "Parish Church" which was "to be placed in the fork." On 9 October

1733, the vestry ordered Rev. John Becket to preach at the "New Church," appointed a sexton and clerk to it and offered Lt. Gov. Spotswood "a place in the New Church for a Seate for himself and his family" (*StMVB*, 10–13). The Great Fork Church served Anglican parishioners until at least 1828.[6]

THE COLONIAL CHURCHES AND CHAPELS OF ST. THOMAS' PARISH

The Germanna Church, ca. 1726–1732

The first Anglican house of worship in what would become St. Thomas' Parish was the Germanna Church. Shortly after the formation of Spotsylvania County in 1721, Lt. Gov. Alexander Spotswood received money from the Virginia Assembly to build a parish church at Germanna. It is not known when the Germanna Church was finished and first used for services. The first pages of the St. George's vestry book are missing between 1723—when the vestry was organized—and 1725, and the road orders do not mention the Germanna Church since roads to the church were described as going to the town. However, a few contemporary records offer some hints: Rev. Hugh Jones, in his *Present State of Virginia* (1724), said that Spotswood "is building a church" at Germanna; and in 1726, Spotswood wrote that the church was almost complete. The church may have been consecrated in 1726 when the vestry hired Rev. Theodosius Staige. [1]

The history of the Germanna Church was brief. Sometime between 16 March 1732 when the St. Mark's vestry ordered repairs on the Germanna Church—for which no payment is recorded in the 1732 accounts—and 13 May 1732 when a new parish church was ordered built, the Germanna Church was destroyed in a fire. On 30 June 1732, the vestry ordered "that the Nailes of the Burnt [Germanna] Church be sould" (*StMVB*, 10–11). Colonel William Byrd, who visited Germanna in September 1732, reported that "There had also been a chapel . . . but some pious people had lately burnt it down, with intent to get another built nearer to their own homes."[2]

The Southwest Mountain Chapel, ca. 1729–1735

The earliest recorded date for the Southwest Mountain Chapel, the second oldest house of worship in St. Thomas' Parish, is 1729.

On 16 June 1729, the St. George's vestry ordered "William Philips be reader at the Mountain Chappel" (*StGVB*, 10–11), and on **3 September 1729**, the Spotsylvania County court ordered a road cleared to the "South West Mountain Chappell."[1] However, Paula Felder implied that the Southwest Mountain Chapel existed as early as 1726: "By 1726 [when Rev. Theodosius Staige was hired by the St. George's vestry], the settlers in the fork of the Rapidan and Rappahannock . . . had established chapels of their own, which added new responsibilities for the vestry and its minister. Even though Staige seems to have been exempted from travelling all the way to the Fork Chapel or the Mountain Chapel—where readers had been assigned—he nonetheless had a stressful amount of territory to cover."[2] Ulysses P. Joyner, Jr. also suggested the Southwest Mountain Chapel—which Joyner identified as the Brick (Middle) Church—was in use before 1729: "Reverend Theodosius Staige, the rector of the Germanna Church . . . patented 1,000 acres on the North Fork of the North Anna in 1727 [*VPB* 13:92]. This tract lies immediately east of the [James] Taylor tract . . . upon which was located the 'Old Brick Church'. . . . There is no known evidence that Staige established the church, but the proximity of his lands lends credence to the theory that he did. Nevertheless, Staige soon left the colony [in 1729]."[3]

There is, however, no evidence that the Southwest Mountain Chapel existed much before 1729. There is nothing about the chapel in the St. George's vestry book from 1726 to June 1729 (the vestry minutes from 1723 to 1725 are missing);[4] and there are no roads ordered to this chapel until **3 September 1729**, whereas, over twenty orders for roads to other houses of worship were issued between 1724 and 1729. But it is strange there was no place of worship closer than the Germanna Church for parishioners in central "Orange" County—an area which had been patented and settled by 1726—until 1729.

On **3 September 1729**, the Spotsylvania County court granted Benjamin Cave's petition to clear a road "from the Walnut Branch on y^e. North Side of Rappadan Down the Ridge & to Cross y^e. Rappadan so Down to the South West Mountain Chappell." On

2 February 1730/31, Cave was granted another petition "to have the road that Comes from black Walnut run a Cross the river to the Mountain Chappel Devided at the river." Anthony Head, who lived near today's Liberty Mills, was appointed overseer of the Rapidan River to Mountain Chapel section of this road.[5] The Black Walnut to Rapidan River section of this road started at Black Walnut Run, a northern branch of Elk Run in "Madison" County,[6] and continued "Down the Ridge & to Cross y^e. Rappadan." This road could approximate Route 622, which crosses the northern branches of Elk Run, passes through high elevations, turns south onto Route 231 and then crosses the Rapidan near Liberty Mills; or from Route 231 to 620 to 616 (also called Cave's Road) to the Rapidan near Cave's Ford. Assuming that the two overseers were assigned sections of approximately equal length, with the Rapidan River the mid-point between Black Walnut Run and the Mountain Chapel, then the Southwest Mountain Chapel was (in whatever direction) about nine miles from the Rapidan in "Orange" County.

Five orders on **1 June 1731, 1 August 1732, 6 September 1732, 7 November 1732** and **6 February 1732/33** describe a road from Robert Beverley's Upper Quarter to the "upper Side of the blew run Just below Beverleys Mill to the Chappell road." This road, petitioned by Robert Beverley and assigned to Anthony Head, ran west-east through part of Beverley's 1729 Octonia Grant of 24,000 acres, which spread in a roughly two-mile wide swath along the southern banks of the Rapidan from Stanardsville in the west to Laurel Run in the east. This huge grant was divided into five quarters (a "quarter" usually meant the owner did not live on the land); Beverley managed one quarter and four overseers—one being Anthony Head—managed the others.[7] The western terminus of this road at Beverley's Upper Quarter was somewhere on the southern border of the Octonia Grant near the "Greene" County line;[8] the mid-point was below Robert Beverley's Mill on Blue Run, which was probably below Liberty Mills on either Route 20 or Route 641;[9] and the eastern terminus, at the "Chappel road," was a road going to the Southwest Mountain Chapel.

It is possible that the main length of the road petitioned by Beverley on **1 June 1731** was the "road 16 miles with six bridges cleared by my own negroes," which was described in the 24 June 1732 appraisal of Beverley's Octonia Grant, and which J. Randolph Grymes, Jr. suggested "was probably a portion of the Mountain Road, present-day Route 641 and Route 609."[10] It is also possible that part of the "Chapple Road" approximated Route 616.

Four **18 February 1734/35**[C] road orders describe a four-part road from the "Chapple Road to the Rapidan Caves ford" to Charles Blunt's lower path (on branches of Maple Run and Beautiful Run in "Madison" County [*VPB* 15:55]) to the fork of Elk Run to Stanton's River. If each section of this road was approximately equal in length, then the "Chapple Road" was about ten miles from Cave's Ford somewhere in "Orange" County. The Chapel Road to Elk Run section of this road was probably part of the same road petitioned by and granted Benjamin Cave on **3 September 1729** and **2 February 1730/31**.

On 9 October 1733, 11 December 1733 and 31 May 1734, the St. Mark's vestry ordered Rev. John Becket to preach "every other Sunday at the Southwest Mountain Chapel till further orders" and paid him extra for "tending" the chapel (*StMVB*, 14–15). It is probably not coincidental that the vestry's repeated orders to Becket to perform his duties at the Southwest Mountain Chapel were followed on **4 June 1734** by a petition granted Robert Slaughter, a vestryman, to clear a road from the minister's residence at the St. Mark's "Glebe in the fork of Rappahannock River [a little north of the Great Fork Church] to the South West Mountain Chappel." This long road, assigned to three overseers, passed through the Island Ford, William Connico's land and John Taliaferro's Catamount Quarter to the "South West Mountains Road." All tithables "from the head of the Mountain Run Downwards" were to assist the overseer assigned to the Catamount to Southwest Mountain Road section. John Taliaferro's Catamount Quarter[11] was located on Lawrence and John Taliaferro's 1719 patent (*VPB* 10:418), which spread along the slopes of Clark Mountain and down the Southwest Mountain Run to the Southwest Mountain Road. (William Connico's patent

[*VPB* 12:485] was on Taliaferro's northeast border.)[12]

That the Southwest Mountain Chapel and the Southwest Mountain Road were used interchangeably in this order means the chapel must have been near this road. The Southwest Mountain Road was the first road ordered cleared by the newly formed Spotsylvania County court on 7 August 1722 p. 4. It was petitioned by Lawrence Taliaferro to pass "from the little [Southwest] mountains to the wilderness bridge." Orange County patents, deeds and road orders confirm that this Southwest Mountain Road approximated Route 20.[13] The Southwest Mountain Road and the Southwest Mountain Run were later shortened to Mountain Road and Mountain Run.[14] (All succeeding mention of the Mountain Road refer to this Southwest Mountain Road.) Two county court orders on **18 February 1734/35[A&B]**, which assigned constables to inspect tobacco plants "from the Southside of the Mountain Road up to the Chappell" and "on the Northside of the Mountain Road from the Wildernes[s] Bridge up to the Chappell," confirm the location of the Southwest Mountain Chapel on or near the (Southwest) Mountain Road.[15]

The **4 June 1734** and **18 February 1734/35[A&B]** orders, which placed the Southwest Mountain Chapel somewhere below the head of Mountain Run near the Southwest Mountain Road (Route 20), do not contradict the general location described in road orders **2 February 1730/31** and **1 June 1731**, which placed the Southwest Mountain Chapel about ten miles from the Rapidan River.

The next road order on **5 November 1734[A]** pinpoints the location of the Southwest Mountain Chapel: "Wee likewise present the overseer of the road from y[e]. South west Mountain Chaple on Fox point Run for not keeping his road in Repair from the s[d]. Chaple to Thomas Chews Mill Run for these two months last past." This road from the Southwest Mountain Chapel to Thomas Chew's Mill Run appeared in another road order on **18 February 1734/35[F]**. Thomas Chew's Mill Run became Madison's Mill Run, or today's Madison Run, after part of the 1723 joint patent of Thomas Chew and Ambrose Madison passed to the Madisons in 1737.[16] Fox Point Run, Fox Point and Fox Point Bridge appear in the road orders ten times between 1726 and 1734, then one final time in 1743.[17] Fox Point Run also appears in a few deeds.

On 7 May 1729, Henry Willis sold Goodrich Lightfoot a parcel of land on the "south side of the South West Mountains" (*SCDB* A:106). A few years later, on 4 April 1732, Goodrich Lightfoot deeded this land to his eldest son, John (*SCDB* B:121). In this and all later deeds, the land was described as 300 acres on the south side of the Southwest Mountains, bordered by a branch called Fox Point Run adjoining Zachary Taylor's line and Capt. Beale's line.[18]

This 300 acres was part of Henry Willis' 10,000 acre patent granted 23 July 1728 (*VPB* 13:266), which ran from the "Louisa" County line up to the Pamunkey River on the southern boundary of land Zachary Taylor's father, James, patented in 1722 (*VPB* 11:149). Willis sold his 10,000 acres in four parts: 3,333 acres "on the East side of the Little [Southwest] Mountains" to Capt. Thomas Beale on 6 August 1728 (*SCDB* A:331); 3,333 acres to Ambrose Madison; 300 acres to Goodrich Lightfoot; and "the remainder [3,034 acres] of the said tract of 10,000 acres" to Thomas Hill on 14 February 1733/34 (*SCDB* B:129). The exact boundaries of these four deeds is not known;[19] however, it is clear from the deeds describing Lightfoot's 300 acres that his land was bordered on the north by Taylor and on the south by Beale. But what contemporary run can be identified as the "branch called Foxpoint Run joyning Zachary Taylor"? Ulysses P. Joyner, Jr.'s map of Orange County patents shows Tomahawk Run, which flows from the west into Pamunkey (River) Creek, dividing the Taylor and Willis patents; and Poorhouse Run, which flows from the south into the Tomahawk-Pamunkey waterway, passing through Willis' patent.[20] Poorhouse Run does not appear in the Spotsylvania or Orange County road orders, in any eighteenth-century deeds, or on any eighteenth and nineteenth-century maps I have examined. Tomahawk Run and Tomahawk Bridge appear a number of times in the road orders, after the last appearance of Fox Point in 1743 as "Tommahaugh Bridge" (24 November 1749 p. 143), "Tomahawk Bridge" (26 April 1750 p. 5) and later as Tomahawk Run and Bridge. Whether Fox Point Run was Poorhouse Run or Tomahawk Run, the road from the "South west Mountain Chaple on Fox point Run . . . to Thomas Chews Mill Run" (**5 November 1734 and 18 February 1734/35**), probably approximated Route 612 crossing Tomahawk Run to Route 637 crossing Poorhouse Run to Route 647 crossing Madison (Thomas Chew's Mill) Run. This road was part of a longer road, Route 15, from the Hanover (today's Louisa) County line to the Mountain Road (Route 20), which is discussed below.

The fact that Goodrich Lightfoot purchased this 300 acres on or near where the Southwest Mountain Chapel stood one month before the earliest mention of this chapel on 16 June 1729, is interesting because Lightfoot, who resided on his 1726 patent (*VPB* 12:484) in southeast "Culpeper" County, was a vestryman of St. George's Parish from 1726 to 1730 (*StGVB*, 2, 15) and St. Mark's Parish from 1731 to 1738 (*StMVB*, 7, 22). Was the chapel already there when Lightfoot purchased the land, or did he purchase it in order to donate or sell part of the land to the parish for the purpose of building a chapel?

The last roads ordered to the Southwest Mountain Chapel on **18 February 1734/35**[E] and **18 March 1734/35**[B] assigned overseers to maintain the "highways from the Tombs Stone to the Chappell Bridge." These are the only references in the road orders to a Chapel Bridge, which later orders identify as a bridge near the Southwest Mountain Chapel. (On **26 June 1760** and **26 November 1763**, a "Church Bridge" appears in the road orders. See *The Middle [Brick] Church*.) Road orders to the Tombstone—a site, up to now, unidentified—are of particular interest because of the light they throw on the location and histories of the Southwest Mountain Chapel, Southwest Mountain Church and the Middle (Brick) Church.

Between 1729 and 1757, "Crawford's Tombstone" appears in ten road orders; and between 1732 and 1800, the "Tombstone" appears in thirty-nine road orders. That the two were the same is confirmed by two orders, which use "Crawford's Tombstone" and "Tombstone" interchangeably **(26 January 1743/44 and 22 November 1744)**.[21] It is not known whether "the Place Called the Tomb Stone" **(28 May 1747[A])** was an actual tombstone or a natural landmark associated, for some reason, with a person named Crawford.[22] The Tombstone does not appear on any eighteenth or nineteenth-century maps nor in any deeds I have examined; its absence in deeds may be because this landmark never featured as a property boundary.

Between 1726 and 1789, the road orders describe a long road, divided midway at the Tombstone, running west-east through "Orange" County. Over the years, the names given the termini of this road changed. The western terminus was called Fox Point, (Southwest Mountain) Chapel Bridge, Southwest Mountain Church and the Middle (Brick) Church; the eastern terminus was called Mountain Road, Taliaferro's Road, Old Mountain Road, Alexander Cummins' and the (Old) Trap. The changing names of the termini of this roughly forty-mile long road are traced below.

• On 1 November 1726 pp. 16–17, a new road was approved from the Hanover County line (near the line dividing today's Albemarle and Louisa Counties) to Fox Point and from "ffox point to Taliaferros road." Thomas Jackson was overseer of the northern section of this road.

• On 4 July 1727 p. 20, John Rucker replaced Thomas Jackson as overseer of the road from "Fox Point to Taliaferros road."

• On 2 October 1728 p. 29, Joseph Hawkins replaced John Rucker as overseer of the road from "Taliaferros road to Fox point bridge."

• On 6 August 1729 pp. 36–37, Joseph Hawkins petitioned for "the South West Mountain Road [to be] Devided into Two Precints . . . from Craffords Tomb Stone." Abraham Bledsoe was assigned the eastern half of this road, and, although not stated, Hawkins was assigned the western half.

• On 2 February 1730/31 p. 50, Henry Downes replaced Joseph Hawkins as overseer of the road from "Taliaferro's road to ffoxs

Point bridge." (This order, unlike those that follow, did not describe the road's division, which was ordered in 1729.)

• On 1 February 1731/32 p. 61, John Davis replaced Henry Downes as overseer of the road from "Crawfords tomb Stone to ffox Point."

• On 2 April 1734 p. 85, George Eastham replaced John Davis as overseer of the road from "Crawfords Tomb Stone to ffoxpoint."

• On **18 February 1734/35[E]**, William Smith was appointed overseer of the road from the "Tombs Stone to the Chappell Bridge." (The first road assignments of the newly formed Orange County court in 1735 made no reference to previous overseers. After this 1735 order, the western terminus of this road was called the [Southwest Mountain] Chapel Bridge, the Southwest Mountain Church and the Middle Church—except on 25 November 1743 p. 92 when it was called, for the last time, Fox Point. Probably because the road from the Hanover County line to Fox Point to Taliaferro's Road predated the earliest documented date of 1729 for the Southwest Mountain Chapel, descriptions of this road from 1729 until the first orders of the newly formed Orange County court used the original 1726 description.)

• On **18 March 1734/35[B]**, John Lightfoot replaced William Smith as overseer of the road from the "Tomb Stone to the Chappel Bridge."

• On 17 June 1735 p. 11, John Rucker replaced the deceased John Lightfoot as overseer of an unnamed road. (John Rucker had been overseer of this road 4 July 1727 p. 20 and had worked on it **7 November 1732**.)

• On **27 April 1738**, Zachary Taylor was appointed overseer of the road from the "[Southwest Mountain] Church to y[e] tombstone." (Overseers were not usually assigned to one road for three years, but there was no order to replace John Rucker, and no one else was assigned to this road between 17 June 1735 p. 11 and **27 April 1738**. Later orders confirm that this road assigned to Taylor is the road under discussion.)

• On 25 November 1743 p. 92, John Lucas replaced Zachary Taylor as overseer of the road from "Fox point bridge to Crawfords Tombstone." (This is an odd reversion to the 2 April 1734 p. 85 road description.)

- On **26 January 1743/44**, John Lucas requested assistance on the "Church to the Tombstone" road.
- On **22 November 1744**, the court charged the "Overseer [John Lucas] of the road from the Middle Church to Crawfords Tomb Stone for not Keeping the said Road in repair."
- On **22 May 1746**, Thomas Newman replaced John Lucas as overseer of the road from the "south west Mountain Church to the Tomstone."
- And on **28 May 1747**[A], the court ordered "the road from the middle Church in S^t: Thomas's Parish to the Place Called the Tomb Stone be Divided." Thomas Newman was assigned to the "Church to Poplar Spring" section and John Finny "the lower part [to the Tombstone]."

These Tombstone road orders provide incontrovertible proof that the "South west Mountain Chaple on Fox point Run," the Southwest Mountain Church and the Middle (Brick) Church were in the vicinity of Tomahawk or Poorhouse (Fox Point) Runs and on what must have been a well-travelled road, which entered the county at the Hanover County line, crossed Thomas Chew's (Madison's) Mill Run, then Fox Point (Tomahawk or Poorhouse) Run and then joined the (Southwest) Mountain Road. This road can be identified, roughly, as today's Routes 15 to 647 to 637 to 612 to 631 to 20.

Later road orders place the Tombstone below Rhoadesville and Route 20 near the junction of Route 650 and Route 20 (see **Appendix II: The Tombstone**). The location of the Tombstone on Route 20 near Rhoadesville, and the identification of Fox Point Run as Tomahawk Run or Poorhouse Run clarifies the **7 November 1732** appeal made by some tithables assigned to the road petitioned by Robert Beverley on **1 June 1731** "to be released and Discharged from the road . . . from the Chappell to the Top of the Hill above blew Water Runk [and Beverley's Mill] Setting forth that they serve on the road from ffox Point to Crawfords Stone Which is Ten or Eleven Miles Distance."

No roads are ordered to the Southwest Mountain Chapel after **18 March 1734/35**[B]. The explanation for what happened to the

Southwest Mountain Chapel is found in the St. Mark's Parish vestry minutes.

On 11 December 1733, the vestry met at the Southwest Mountain Chapel and ordered John Lightfoot, William Phillips and John Rucker to find a place "Convenent to the Southwest Mountain Road with in a Mile of the first run [presumably, Fox Point] below the [Southwest Mountain] Chapel" for another parish church. David Kinked, who had completed the construction of the Great Fork Church—the first parish church built in St. Mark's Parish—in August 1733, was hired to build this second parish church at a cost of 27,900 pounds of tobacco (Great Fork Church cost 36,000 pounds of tobacco). He was to have it ready for prayers by December 1734 and completed by December 1735 (*StMVB*, 14–15). At the same vestry meeting on 11 December 1733, the vestry ordered Benjamin Cave to find a place "near Mr. Mosly Batleys quarter" to build a small chapel; and on 10 October 1734, Thomas Jackson was paid 2,800 pounds of tobacco for building this "Chapel at the Southwest Mountain" (*StMVB*, 14–15, 53; see *The Upper Chapel*.)

The vestry minutes do not explicitly say what happened to the Southwest Mountain Chapel, and between 10 October 1734 and 10 October 1735 the minutes are confusing. However, the annual assignment of readers and sextons to the parish churches and chapels clarify what occurred in the parish at this time.

The St. George's and the St. Mark's vestry minutes record William Phillips as reader at the "Southwest Mountain Chapel" (also called the "Mountain Chapel") from 16 June 1729 until 9 October 1733 (*StGVB*, 10, 16; *StMVB*, 7, 14, 51–52). On 10 October 1734, Phillips was ordered to "be continued Reader at the uper Chapel" in 1735 (also called the "Mountain Chapel" and the "Chapel" in the vestry minutes),[23] and the vestry ordered David Cave to be paid 435 pounds of tobacco for having read six times at an unnamed house of worship and to "be continued Reader at the Mountain Chapel for this insuing year" (*StMVB*, 16). On the next day, 11 October 1734, the vestry ordered Samuel Drake, who had served as sexton at the Southwest Mountain Chapel since first assigned on 9 October 1733, to continue as sexton at the "Mountain Chapel" (*StMVB*, 13, 14, 16). In spite of this confusing use of "Mountain Chapel" to describe both the Upper Chapel—built by Thomas Jackson and assigned to William Phillips—and the Southwest Mountain Chapel, the vestry's 10 and 11 October 1734 orders clearly show that William Phillips became reader at the Upper Chapel, and David Cave replaced Phillips as reader at the Southwest Mountain Chapel sometime around May 1734. (In October, Cave was paid for reading five months at an unnamed house of worship and was ordered to continue as reader at the Southwest Mountain Chapel—just as, on the same day, Phillips was ordered to continue at the Upper Chapel.) David Cave and Samuel Drake, reader and sexton, respectively, at the Southwest Mountain Chapel and later the "church at the Mountains" (the Southwest Mountain Church), continued in these positions until at least 1740 when St. Thomas' Parish was formed (*StMVB*, 19, 20, 22, 24, 26, 54–57).[24]

Therefore, sometime between **18 March 1734/35**[B] when the last road order mentioned the Southwest Mountain Chapel and **16 September 1735**[B] when the first road order mentioned the "Mountain Church," the Southwest Mountain Chapel was replaced by the nearby Southwest Mountain Church, which the vestry had ordered David Kinked to have ready for services December 1734 and completed December 1735. After 1735, the Southwest Mountain Chapel disappeared from the St. Mark's vestry minutes and the Orange Country court order books. Whether this chapel, which had been built about six years earlier in the vicinity of Route 637 and Tomahawk Run or Poorhouse Run, continued to be used as a chapel of ease, was simply abandoned or was torn down is not known.

The Southwest Mountain Church, 1735–1744

Based on the evidence presented in the previous section, the Southwest Mountain Church, the second parish church ordered built by the St. Mark's vestry, replaced the nearby Southwest Mountain Chapel sometime between **18 March 1734/35**[B] and 16

September 1735[B]—much like the first parish church, the Great Fork Church, replaced the nearby Fork Chapel in 1733. The Southwest Mountain Church was built where the Middle Church—the new name given to the Southwest Mountain Church in 1744 (see below)—is unanimously agreed to have stood: below the Southwest Mountain Road (Route 20) in the fork of Routes 612 and 631, below a slight elevation later called "Church Hill" and near the mouth of Church Run.[1] This location was less than a mile northeast of the mouth of Tomahawk Run (Fox Point Run?), which agrees with the 11 December 1733 vestry order to build the Southwest Mountain Church "Convenent to the Southwest Mountain Road with in a Mile of the first run below the [Southwest Mountain] Chapel" (*StMVB*, 14–15).

The new parish church was called the "Southwest Mountain Church," the "Church at the Southwest Mountains," the "Church at the Mountains," the "Mountain Church," the "Parish Church" or, simply, the "Church" in the vestry minutes and road orders.[2] Although nothing is known about the physical appearance of this church, it may have resembled—on a less grand scale—two churches commissioned by the St. George's vestry in 1731 at a total cost of 75,000 pounds of tobacco (27,000 was paid for the Southwest Mountain Church). Each church was to measure sixty by twenty-four feet, be constructed of wood with a brick foundation, have a gabled roof and ten windows "of Good Crown Glass from London" and be painted white on the interior and exterior (*StGVB*, 23, 24).

From 1735 to 1740 when St. Thomas' Parish was formed, the St. Mark's vestry ordered David Cave and Samuel Drake to serve as reader and sexton, respectively, at the "Mountain Church;" and they ordered workers to clean the spring and yard around the church, to "Tar the Mountain Church and make hors Blocks and Benches and hooks for the wendows . . . and Ladles and Chains for the springs" and to glaze and finish the church's windows (*StMVB*, 20, 22–24).

Only a few roads ordered to the Southwest Mountain Church reveal anything of interest. There are several orders to maintain older roads which had gone to the Southwest Mountain Chapel from the Island Ford (**16 September 1735^B**) and from the Tombstone (**27 April 1738, 26 January 1743/44, 22 May 1746**). A 25 March 1742^B order for a "road from David Caves Church path" is interesting because it probably describes a path which joined a road to the Southwest Mountain Chapel and Church used by David Cave, lay reader at the Chapel and Church for, at least, six years.

There were some new roads petitioned and granted to the Southwest Mountain Church: from James Coward's (**26 May 1743^A**), from Richard Thomas' Quarter (**18 November 1735**),[3] from "the Mouth of ye Robinson" (**28 May 1741, 26 June 1741, 27 May 1742^B**), a long road granted to the "Inhabitants of Pomunkey" on **27 September 1739** from Pleasant Run near the Spotsylvania County border "to about three miles from the Church thence the nighest way into the mountain road"[4] and a "Bridle way from their Neighbourhood to the Mountain Church" granted John Ingram and Thomas Sims (**22 May 1740, 28 November 1740**).[5]

On **22 November 1744**, a road previously described as going to the Southwest Mountain Church was described as going to the "Middle Church;" on **22 May 1746**, the same road was again described as going to the Southwest Mountain Church; and on **28 May 1747^A**, this road was described as going to "the middle Church in St: Thomas's Parish." The name "Southwest Mountain Church" disappeared from the road orders after 1746. It is unlikely that the new name, Middle Church, given to the Southwest Mountain Church—less than a decade after it was built—meant that it was torn down and replaced with a new church. A possible reason for the renaming of the Southwest Mountain Church is offered below in *The Middle (Brick) Church.*

The Upper Chapel, 1734–?

At the 11 December 1733 St. Mark's vestry meeting when the vestry ordered the construction of the Southwest Mountain Church, they also ordered Benjamin Cave to select a site "near

Mr. Mosly Batleys quarter convenant to the best spring" and to hire "the Chepest work Man" to build a twenty-foot square chapel (*StMVB*, 15). On 10 October 1734, the vestry paid Thomas Jackson 2,800 pounds of tobacco for building "a Chapel at the Southwest Mountain" ("Chapel at the Mountains" in the 1734 accounts; *StMVB*, 14–15, 53). The modest cost of 2,800 pounds of tobacco would be fitting for the small chapel Cave had been ordered to arrange.[1] On 10 October 1734, William Phillips was appointed reader at this new chapel, now called the "uper Chapel" (*StMVB*, 16). It appears there was no sexton at this new chapel until the vestry ordered Charles Blunt to take up the post on 8 October 1736 (*StMVB*, 20). Phillips and Blunt served at the Upper Chapel until at least 1740, after which record of their service is lost with the missing St. Thomas' Parish vestry books. Between 1734 and 1740, this chapel is called the "Chapel at the Southwest Mountains," the "Chapel at the Mountains," the "Mountain Chapel," the "uper Chapel" or the "Chapel" in the St. Mark's vestry minutes (*StMVB*, 15–21, 53–56). In the road orders it is simply called the "Chapel" or "old Chappell." (A later and different "upper Church" appears **25 November 1743**, see *The Upper Church*.)

The location of "Mr. Mosly Batleys" quarter and the Upper Chapel are difficult to pinpoint. (The name of this "Mosly Batley" is written a myriad of ways, but most eighteenth-century documents show it spelled Mosley or Moseley Battaley.) On 28 March 1733, a patent of 500 acres in the first fork of the Rapidan adjoining Michael Holt and John Rucker was granted Elizabeth Battaley, widow of Robert Taliaferro and wife of Mosley Battaley (*VPB* 15:8). On the same day, another (adjoining?) patent of 1,482 acres adjoining the properties of Holt, Rucker and Mosley Battaley was granted the infants Elizabeth and Mary Taliaferro. On 16 June 1738, the 1,482 acres of the Taliaferro children passed to Mosley Battaley (*VPB* 18:20).

The location of the property of Mosley Battaley's neighbors provides clues to the location of Battaley's property. John Rucker and Michael Holt lived on the southern edge of the Robinson River Valley German community below White Oak

(Island) Run (*VPB* 13:162, 294). A 1743 road order instructed all tithables between Robinson River and Smith Run—a branch of Beautiful Run south of Platts[2]—and Michael Holt's tithables, to work on a road from Eddin's Ford on the Rapidan River to Mr. Battaley's Quarter (26 March 1743 p. 83). William Eddin's 400 acre patent was near Neal's Mountain adjoining Holt and Rucker (*VPB* 14:246, 15:135). This places Battaley's Quarter in "Madison" County someplace south of White Oak (Island) Run and east of the Rapidan. This general location in southern "Madison" County for the site of the Upper Chapel is supported by the residences of the builder, reader and sexton of the new chapel: Thomas Jackson owned 1000 acres on the Rapidan River and Elk Run (*VPB* 13:159, 458), William Phillips had extensive acreage in the area of Elk and Beautiful Runs (*VPB* 15:137, 139, 502, 514) and Charles Blunt owned 200 acres on Maple and Beautiful Runs (*VPB* 15:55).

Only two Orange County court orders describe roads to the Upper Chapel and both require some background information to understand them. In 1733, Jonathan Gibson's petition on behalf of "the Inhabitants of the Great [Blue Ridge] Mountains" for a road from "Ruckers Road . . . to Offills Mountain" was granted, and Thomas Jackson was appointed overseer (7 August 1733 p. 79). Dewey Lillard identified Offill's Mountain as Goodall Mountain, which is above Stanardsville in the north of Greene County. Lillard also suggested Rucker's Road was in south Madison County and ran from the head of Garth's Run to Wolftown to below Shelby to the Rapidan; part of this road approximates Route 662 from Wolftown to Shelby.[3] Three 1734 orders (6 March 1733/34 p. 85, 7 May 1734 p. 87, 4 June 1734 p. 87) addressed a disagreement between Gibson and Jackson about this road's route, which the court resolved when they ordered Jackson to clear the road from Rucker's Road (Route 662) "over the foot of Neals Mountain . . . to the foot of offields Mountain" (Route 663 starts at Route 662, passes north of Neal's Mountain and westward toward Offill's Mountain). On **18 February 1734/35**[D], at the second meeting of the newly formed Orange County court when the court reaffirmed or reassigned road orders of the Spotsylvania court, Thomas Jackson was appointed overseer of the road "from the Chappel to the foot of Offells Mountain." The fact that four months earlier, on 10 October 1734, Jackson was paid for building the Upper Chapel may explain why "the Chappel" now replaced "Ruckers Road" as the name of the eastern terminus of this road to Offill's Mountain. In 1738, John Rogers replaced Jackson as overseer of "Gibsons road from Ruckers [Road] to the Offill Mountain" (23 March 1737/38 p. 29). In this order, the road from Rucker's Road (or, "the Chappel") to Offill's Mountain is now called Gibson's Road after the man who petitioned the road in 1733. Route 663 follows the course described for this Gibson's Road: starting at Rucker's Road (Route 662) and passing north of Neal's Mountain toward Offill's Mountain. These road orders, then, place the Upper Chapel near the junction of Routes 662 and 663.

In 1737, Thomas Jackson was granted his petition for a road from his mill to Gibson's Road, and Richard Mauldin was appointed overseer (22 May 1737 p. 23). On **29 January 1742/43**[A], Thomas Jackson, Jr. replaced Mauldin as overseer of the "road from the old Chappell to Jacksons Mill," and in 1747, James Rucker replaced Jackson, Jr. as the overseer of the road from Jackson's Mill to Gibson's Road (28 May 1747 p. 130). In these three orders, the name of this road's terminus alternated between Gibson's Road and the Upper Chapel (as the previous orders alternated between Rucker's Road and the Upper Chapel). (Although it is strange that a chapel built less than ten years previously was called "old," the St. Mark's vestry minutes mention no other chapel in this area at this time except the Upper Chapel.) Since Thomas Jackson's Mill was on Elk Run,[4] which flows into the Rapidan above Burtonville, this new road ran from someplace on Elk Run up to Gibson's Road (or the Upper Chapel). Route 621 runs from the Rapidan along branches of Elk Run and joins Route 662 (Rucker's Road) a little east of the junction of Route 663 (Gibson's Road). The location of the Upper Chapel in the high elevations where Routes 621 and 663 join Route 662, a little west of Shelby, would fit the chapel's description as a "Mountain Chapel"—but not a "Chapel at the Southwest Mountains" as appeared in the St. Mark's vestry book on 10 October 1734.

Although information about the Upper Chapel is sparse, the St. Mark's vestry orders date its construction to sometime between 11 December 1733 when Benjamin Cave was ordered to find a good location for this chapel on Mosley Battaley's Quarter and 10 October 1734 when Thomas Jackson was paid for building the chapel and William Phillips was appointed reader at the new chapel. Deeds place Mosley Battaley's Quarter (and the residences of the builder, reader and sexton of the chapel) in southern "Madison" County, and road orders narrow the location to a little west of Shelby where Routes 621 and 663 join Route 662. The later history of the Upper Chapel is not known. After the formation of Culpeper County in 1749, the Upper Chapel—though it would remain part of St. Thomas' Parish until Bromfield Parish was formed in 1752—was no longer in the area covered by the Orange County road orders.[5] It is curious that this chapel is mentioned in only two road orders between 1735 and 1750.

The Formation of St. Thomas' Parish, 1740

That from and after the first day of November next [1740], the said parish of St. Mark shall be divided by a line, to be run from the Wilderness bridge, up the Mountain road to the head of Russell run; thence down the said run to the river Rappidan; thence up the Rappidan, to the Robinson River and thence, from the said river, along the ridge, between the Robinson and Rappidan, to the top of the Blue Ridge of mountains; and all that part of the said parish, situate on their north side of the said bounds, be erected into one distinct parish, and retain the name of St. Mark; and all that other part thereof, situate on the south side of the said bounds, be erected into one other distinct parish, and called by the name of Saint Thomas (*StMVB*, 1–2).

When St. Thomas' Parish was formed in 1740, it encompassed the counties of present day Orange, Greene and a strip of southern

Madison. The exact division between the parishes of St. Mark and St. Thomas in "Madison" County is not clear since there is no easily identifiable east-west ridge "from the said [Robinson] river . . . between the Robinson and Rappidan, to the top of the Blue Ridge of mountains." But the fact that there was no mention of the Upper Chapel in the St. Mark's vestry book after 1740 means the Chapel was inside the boundaries of St. Thomas' Parish, and the line through "Madison" County must have run above the Upper Chapel, which was in the vicinity of today's Shelby (see *The Upper Chapel*).

From the formation of St. Thomas' Parish in 1740 until 18 May 1749 when Culpeper County was formed from Orange County, the Orange County court was responsible for roads to the churches, chapels and glebes in both St. Mark's and St. Thomas' Parishes. From 1750, the Orange County court's jurisdiction was reduced to today's Orange and Greene Counties. However, this means the Orange County court's jurisdiction did not encompass all of St. Thomas' Parish, which extended—until 1752 when Bromfield Parish was formed—into southern "Madison" County: roads in this part of St. Thomas' Parish were the responsibility of the Culpeper County court.

The formation of St. Thomas' Parish reduced the number of tithables in St. Mark's Parish from 2,107 in 1740 to 979 in 1741 (*StMVB*, 28, 31)[2] and left St. Mark with only the Great Fork Church, the Little Fork Chapel and the North Chapel. St. Thomas' Parish took the Southwest Mountain Church and Upper Chapel and two of the twelve St. Mark's vestrymen, Benjamin Cave and James Barbour. Unfortunately, the vestry minutes of St. Thomas' Parish were lost and with them the names and tenure of ministers, vestrymen, lay readers and sextons and orders for the construction of new churches and chapels. Some of this information can be recovered from the Orange County court orders, which are a particularly valuable source of information for the houses of worship built by the St. Thomas' vestry—the Upper Church, the Pine Stake Church and the New (Orange) Church—as well as the names of some vestrymen and Anglican and dissenting ministers.[3]

Upon the formation of a new parish, the vestry was legally required to purchase no less than 200 acres of land and furnish it with a house and other buildings for the use of the parish minister. This minister's residence, the glebe, provided the parish minister with a working farm to satisfy his needs.[4] In 1743, Elijah and Mary Daniel, of Caroline County, sold Edward Spencer and James Coleman, church wardens of St. Thomas' Parish, 307 acres in northwest "Orange" County near Glebe Run and today's Route 634 for use as a glebe (*OCDB* 9:52).[5] Although no description remains of the St. Thomas' glebe, it probably had the same buildings the St. George's and St. Mark's vestries ordered built on their glebes: a house with cellar, a corn house, stable, meat house, kitchen and dairy.[6] Road orders reveal that the minister's "Glebe hands"—slaves and/or indentured servants—were not exempt from working on the roads (24 November 1737 p. 27, 28 June 1745 p. 111).

Rev. Joseph Earnest said that Rev. James Marye, Jr., minister of St. Thomas' Parish from 1760 to 1768, was "the first minister in St. Thomas Parish whose residence we can with any degree of certainty fix at the glebe."[7] However, the St. Thomas' glebe dated much earlier. On **26 July 1750** and **26 June 1755**[A], Rev. Mungo Marshall, minister of St. Thomas' Parish from ca. 1750 to 1757, petitioned "for a Road to be cleared from the Gleebe . . . the Most convenientest way for his going to the Upper Church." But an even earlier order on **23 January 1745/46** for a "road from the Glebe in Saint Marks Parrish" could indicate that with two glebes in the county, it was necessary to distinguish one from the other. It is likely that the St. Thomas' glebe was ready for habitation in at least 1746, three years after the glebe land was purchased.[8]

The Upper Church, ca. 1742–After 1800

On **27 May 1742**[A], less than two years after the formation of St. Thomas' Parish, the court granted Alexander Cleveland's petition for a road "from the New Church into Anthony Heads road." On **26 February 1742/43** and **27 May 1743**[B], the court ordered this new road to be cleared "out of the James River Mountain road near or about Head Lynch's house to go by the Arbour ["ye harbour" in the May order] the nearest & Best way that is to be found into Anthony Heads road about half a mile below ye Church." Since the 1743 orders described "Anthony Heads road about half a mile below ye Church," the 1742 petition for a road "from the New Church into Anthony Heads road" was miswritten; the petitioned road was probably from the vicinity of the petitioner's home to this New Church. The residence of Alexander Cleveland and the "Arbour" or "harbour" are not easy to fix, but Head Lynch's house and Anthony Head's Road can be identified. Head Lynch patented 400 acres in 1736 near today's Albano.[1] Anthony Head's Road appears several times in the road orders—usually as "Heads road"—from **27 May 1742**[A] to 1747. Roads often took the name of their overseer,[2] and Head's Road was probably the road Anthony Head was ordered to clear and oversee on **1 June 1731** from Robert Beverley's Upper Quarter to Beverley's Mill to the (Southwest Mountain) Chapel Road (Routes 609 and 641 or 20). Therefore, at least part of this new road ran through the vicinity of Albano (Route 644) up to Head's Road (Route 609), and the New Church was between Head's Road and the Rapidan.

On **25 November 1743**, a road "from Blue run Road to ye upper Church" was ordered repaired. Subsequent roads ordered to this Upper Church identify it as the "New Church" above Head's Road described in the 1742 and 1743 orders. Of the twenty-two orders for roads to the Upper Church, only a few offer clues to its location. On **28 April 1763**[B], a rolling road was petitioned "out of the Road near Braxtons old Quarter to come into the Road that goes by the Church Near the Red Oake Level." One month later, the description of this proposed road was rephrased: "a Road to be cleared out of the Road by Braxtons old Quarter into the Swift run road by the Red Oak Level" (May 1763 p. 84). An earlier order described "the road Called Heads Road at the Red Oak Levell" (23 May 1745 p. 108). Thus, the Upper Church was above Swift Run Road (Head's Road) near the Red Oak Level. Swift Run Road was the primary county road, which ran from Swift Run Gap to Stanardsville (Route 33) to Scuffletown to Old Somerset (Route 609) to Orange and onto Fredericksburg (Route 20).[3] The location of the Red Oak Level[4]—a flat plot of land covered with red oaks, which was large enough to be remarkable in this hilly and mountainous region—is revealed in the road orders. On **24 January 1750/51**[B] and **26 October 1758**, a bridge was ordered built "over the Beverdam run below the upper Church." Route 609 crosses Beaver Run less than a mile east of the junction of Routes 609 and 644. Route 644, suggested above as approximating the new road petitioned by Alexander Cleveland on **27 May 1742**[A], joins Route 609 at unusually level terrain—arguably, the Red Oak Level. Therefore, these road orders place the Upper Church between the Rapidan River and Route 609 (Head's Road, Swift Run Road), above Beaver Run and near the Red Oak Level, which was probably in the vicinity of the junction of Routes 644 and 609.

Anthony Head's Road, the Red Oak Level and this new Upper Church were within the boundaries of Robert Beverley's Octonia Grant. An advertisement for the sale of the Octonia Grant, in the 2 February 1769 issue of the *Virginia Gazette*, described the property as "having one church and four mills upon it."[5] This "one church" can only be the Upper Church. (There was no mention of a church on Beverley's Octonia Grant when his land was appraised in 1732.)[6] The construction of the Upper Church in ca. 1742, shortly after the formation of St. Thomas' Parish, added one more church to the existing Southwest Mountain Church and Upper Chapel in the new parish of St. Thomas.

On **24 January 1744/45, 27 June 1745** and **22 August 1745** a petition was granted and a route approved for a road from the "New Church Road into blue Run Road a little above the three Springs." Since nine men—more than usual—were ordered to clear and set up "posts of Direction if Necessary" on this road, it must have been a long road. The location of the "three Springs" is not known, but many of the people assigned to this new road worked on the **27 May 1742**[A] road petitioned by Alexander Cleveland to the New Church. This "New Church Road" was probably a new road to the Upper Church rather than *a road to a new church*. (The Upper Church was called the "New Church" in only the **27 May 1742^A** order.)

The road "from Blue run Road to ye upper Church," first assigned on **25 November 1743**, is important to trace because the final order for this road "from the blue run to the old church" on **28 October 1794**, establishes that sometime between **26 October 1758** and **27 October 1774^A** the Upper Church started to be called the "Old Church." The transfer of responsibility from one overseer to another between 1742 and 1800 traces the changing name of the eastern terminus of this road from "Blue run Road" to "Blue Run" to "Henry Downs's" to "the Main road above Beverleys Mill" to "fork of the Road by Wilsons Store" [7] then back to "blue run." [8] The eastern terminus of this road to the Upper (Old) Church was probably where Route 20 crosses Blue Run below today's Liberty Mills (near Beverley's Mill, see p. 100n. 9). From **22 March 1749/50** to **23 April 1793^F**, the westward continuation of this road was ordered from the Upper (Old) Church to "Heads Ford" or "the great run Bridge" or "Burton's Mill run." [9] The location of Head's Ford is not known. Great (Big, White) Run flows parallel to Route 609 from Burtonville to near Dawsonville where it crosses Route 609 to join the Rapidan. May Burton purchased 340 acres of the Octonia Grant between 1769 and 1779 on the south side of the Rapidan; Route 609 and the Great Run, up to where it joins the Rapidan, ran through his land. [10] (Was Great Run called Burton's Mill Run when May Burton owned the land?) The western terminus of this road appears to have been in northeast "Greene" County where Great Run (Burton's Mill Run) crosses Route 609 (Swift Run Road) near the Rapidan.

Three other roads ordered to the Upper Church are worth noting. On **26 July 1750**, Rev. Mungo Marshall, minister of St. Thomas' Parish, petitioned for a road "from the Glebe by M^r. Tinsleys over the mouth of Baylors Run into the Main Road that leads by Capt. Downs Mill ["into the Road that go's to Beverleys Mill" on the **26 June 1755^A** order granting the petition] as the most convenient way for the Neighbours by him to pass to the uper Church & to the said Mill." The glebe, Marshall's residence, was southeast of Madison Mills near Route 634. This road may have passed down the east side of the Rapidan to Beverley's Mill (below Liberty Mills) where it joined Route 609 to the Upper Church. Another road, ordered by the court on **22 February 1753**, was to be cleared "out of the Road below William Lucas Junr. over the Marsh Run the Most Convenientest way to the upper Church." William Lucas owned land on Marsh Run (*VPB* 17:35), which flows northeast from Greene County and, with Beaver Run, joins the Rapidan near the junction of Routes 609 and 644.

The last road to consider is a **23 June 1748** court order to "view the Way from the River to the upper Church in Saint Thomas's Parish through the Lands of Darby Quin & to report to the Court the most convenient way for a Bridle Way." J. William Browning, Orange County Clerk from 1919 to 1936, was the only historian to recognize the existence of the Upper Church and place it in northwest "Orange" County. He said, "The Clerk of Upper Church of St. Thomas Parish used to travel between Darby Quinn's Plantation and the River—it was used as a 'horse way'. This plantation is where Beautiful Run empties into the Rapidan River. He used this to go from his house to the Church. There is mention of Mr. Quinn erecting a barrier at some point and the clerk petitioning to get the barrier removed because he had to go out of his way to go around the plantation."[11] The **23 June 1748** road order made no mention of a clerk of the Upper Church requesting this bridle-way. In Browning's list of church personages compiled from Orange County court records, he noted a "Robert Sharman . . . 1748 (Clerk of Upper Church of St. Thomas Parish petition about horse way)."[12] Browning probably found this reference to Sharman in an earlier untranscribed court order, which recorded Robert Sharman's petition for this road. Robert Sharman's land on the north bank of the Rapidan in southern "Madison" County must have adjoined or been very close to Darby Quinn's land, which lay between Sharman's house and the Upper Church.[13]

The **23 June 1748** order is also interesting because the location of the Upper Church is specified as being "in Saint Thomas's Parish." Such a qualifier appears in the Orange County road orders only two other times; like this order they appear in the 1740s, the decade when the Orange County court was responsible for roads to parish buildings in both St. Mark's and St. Thomas' Parishes (between the formation of St. Thomas' Parish in 1740 and the formation of Culpeper County, which became responsible for St. Mark's Parish, in 1750). On **23 January 1745/46**, the court probably specified that the road ordered was to the "Glebe in Saint Marks Parrish" because there was also a glebe in St. Thomas. And on **28 May 1747**[A], the Middle Church was probably described as being in "S^t: Thomas's Parish" because "Middle Church" was the new name which had been only recently given to the Southwest Mountain Church. But why did the court specify the "upper Church in Saint Thomas's Parish" in this **23 June 1748** order? This church had been called the Upper Church in the road orders since **25 November 1743**, and there is no mention of another Upper Church in the St. Mark's vestry minutes.

The Upper (Old) Church appears in the published Orange County road orders up to 1800. Hints about the fate of this church, which was built ca. 1742 in northwest "Orange" County in the vicinity of the junction of today's Routes 644 and 609, might appear in a local tradition about a church in northwest "Orange" County taken over by a Baptist congregation and later used as a granary. This is discussed below in **The Historians of Colonial St. Thomas' Parish**.

The Middle (Brick) Church, 1744–Early 1800s

In 1744, the nine-year-old Southwest Mountain Church, which stood in the fork of today's Routes 612 and 631 near the mouth of Church Run, was renamed the Middle Church (see above, p. 24). The Middle Church and the Southwest Mountain Church have never been identified as the same church.[1] However, Ulysses P. Joyner, Jr. came closest to recognizing the connection between the two churches and the Southwest Mountain Chapel when he suggested that Rev. Theodosius Staige, the first minister of St. George's Parish (1726–1729), who patented land east of

James Taylor's patent "upon which was located 'The Old Brick Church' . . . established the church or served its pulpit." He added, that although "there is no known evidence" to prove it, "the close proximity of his patent to the church lends credence to the contention that he did."[2] The Southwest Mountain Church was probably renamed "Middle Church" in accordance with the practice of other Virginia parishes of calling the main parish church, the Middle Church.[3]

Sometime between **25 November 1762** and **24 November 1768**[B], the Middle Church was renamed the "Brick Church." ("Brick Church" first appeared in a **24 November 1768**[B] road order; but on **27 June 1771**, "Middle Church" appeared one last time, much like when the Southwest Mountain Church was renamed the Middle Church on **22 November 1744** but reappeared a last time as the Southwest Mountain Church on **22 May 1746**.) It is not known if the Middle Church, which was over thirty years old in 1768—assuming it was not rebuilt in 1744—was simply given a new brick façade or was demolished and rebuilt on or near the site of the Middle Church.[4] The Brick Church is said to have stood until 1806 or 1812 when it was looted and torn down.[5] "The site of the old Brick Church could be clearly identified by scattered bricks as late as 1965. In 1933, bricks from the old church site were placed at the threshold of the present St. Thomas' Church."[6]

A number of road orders describe a Pamunkey Road below, by or to the Middle Church; "the fork of the pamunkey Road below the Church;" and more specifically, "the Pamunky Road about a Mile below the Church."[7] The Pamunkey Road first appeared in the road orders in 1733 and was described as passing from the Mountain Road (Route 20), crossing Beaverdam Run (Clear Creek) and Pleasant Run to Stoney Run Bridge and the Spotsylvania County line (3 October 1733 pp. 80–81).[8] Civil War maps label Route 629 "Pamunkey Road."[9] If the Pamunkey Road in these orders was equivalent to Route 629, it would have passed above, not "below the Middle Church." Either the mid-eighteenth-century Pamunkey Road followed a slightly different route than that of Route 629—possibly a more southerly route closer to the course of the Pamunkey River—or the orders mistakenly described the road as passing below, not above, the church.

Fifty-two roads were ordered cleared and maintained to the Middle (Brick) Church between 1744 and 1797.[10] Although these orders add no new information about the undisputed location of the Middle (Brick) Church in the angle of Church Run and Routes 631 and 612,[11] several are interesting because they describe the topography near the church. A Church Run and one or more bridges near the Middle Church are mentioned in orders between 1752 and 1793.[12] Today, there are two Church Runs in Orange County: one in the northwest below the suggested site of the Upper Church and another, which flows into Pamunkey Creek near where the Middle Church stood. (Also, Pamunkey River is labeled "Church Run" on a Civil War map.)[13] There are also seven orders to build or repair a bridge over the Church Run by the Middle (Brick) Church. The fact that the first order, which mentioned this bridge (**27 February 1752**), directed it to "be rebuilt or repaired at the County Charge," means this bridge was not new and was so large, the county—not the overseer—funded the necessary work. There is no evidence the Southwest Mountain Chapel Bridge (**18 February 1734/35^{E}**) and the Middle Church Bridge spanned the same run and, if so, at the same place.

Another group of interesting orders, between 1757 and 1793, mention a "Hill on the South side of the Run below the Middle Church," "foot of the hill above the Church," "Top of the hill Above the Church run," "Old Chapell Hill" and "Old Chapple Hill by Orange Courthouse."[14] Although these orders place this hill both above and below the Middle (Brick) Church, and the "Old Chapell Hill" was described one time as being by the Orange Courthouse, this is probably the "Church Hill" in the fork of Routes 631 and 612, which appears on an Orange County Civil War map,[15] and which W. W. Scott described as "the hill near [the Middle Church] where the Pamunkey road crosses Church Run."[16] Three other orders in the 1790s describe a "road Below the Courthouse down to Chinch hall," "by Orange Court

Court house then from (illegible) Chinch (?) Hall" and a "road below the CtHouse to the lane Below Ch Hall." These are probably miswritings of "Church Hill."[17]

Other roads to the Middle (Brick) Church were ordered from Poplar Spring" on **23 May 1751**[A], Cave's Ford on **23 May 1751**[B] (probably the same road ordered cleared to the Southwest Mountain Chapel on **3 September 1729**), the Wilderness on **27 October 1794**[B], Mrs. Burnley's on **24 February 1795**, Brockman's Bridge on **27 October 1794**[A] and **25 September 1797**[A], and from Stark's Bridge on **24 May 1750, 22 May 1755** and **26 June 1755**[B].[18]

The Pine Stake Church, ca. 1746–Early to Mid-1800s

The Pine Stake Church first appears in the road orders on **26 September 1746**. Historians have dated its construction 1740–1745 or 1750–1758.[1] J. William Browning said, "it was built prior to 1743, as an old petition in the Clerk's Office of that date refers to it."[2] Joseph Earnest said the Pine Stake Church was standing as late as 1813, and Ann Miller said it "is believed to have fallen to ruin some time in the early or mid-19th century."[3]

The name of this church seems certain to have come from a place called the Pine Stake,[4] which appears often in the road orders from 1723 to 1785. Ulysses P. Joyner, Jr. noted a 1738 deed describing 100 acres "commonly known by the name of the Pine Stake," which he placed north of Route 20 on Route 602. But he said, "There is no indication that the 'Pine Stake Church' was located on the parcel known as the 'Pine Stake'."[5] However, four orders for two roads described these two places being, at least, very near each other: "Road from Bryan Sissons Low grounds to the said pine Stake" (25 March 1762 p. 76) and "road from Bryan Sissons to the Pine Stake Church" (**25 October 1770**[A]), "Road from the pine Stake to Wears Old houses" (26 May 1768 pp. 108–09) and "Road below the Pine Stake Church to the fork at Wares Old houses" (**24 November 1768**[A]).

Between 1746 and 1785, ten or twelve orders describe roads to the Pine Stake Church, but none of these orders pinpoint the exact location of this church. Two late eighteenth-century deeds mention a "Pine Stake Church Road" joining or north of the "Main Mountain Road" (Route 20) (*OCDB* 19:427) and a "Road leading from the Pine Stake Church to the Old Office" (*OCDB* 19:184, 488, 490). Route 602 is labeled the "Office Road" on an Orange County Civil War map.[6] It is likely that the eighteenth-century "Pine Stake Church Road" is today's Pine Stake Road (Route 621), and the intersection of Routes 621 and 602 might be the "fork of the Road below the Pine Stake Church" (**24 November 1768**[A], **25 May 1769, 22 May 1783** and possibly **23 April 1793**[B]). Although Joyner said the Pine Stake Church's "exact location has not been pinpointed," the location north of Rhoadesville at the intersection of Routes 621 (Pine Stake Road) and 602, suggested by Joyner and Miller, agrees with available evidence.[7]

The New (Orange) Church, ca. 1761–1800s

Eighteen years after the last mention of the "(Upper) Chapel" in the road orders and eleven years after roads to the Upper Chapel became the responsibility of the newly formed Culpeper County, the Orange County court ordered two roads cleared to a chapel. William Bell was granted a petition to clear a "Bridle Way from his house to the Chappel" (**28 May 1761, 24 July 1761, 28 October 1762**), and a road was ordered "cleared from the Chapple to Join the Road Cleared by Culpeper County Near Conways Quarter" (**24 March 1763**[B], **28 April 1763**[A]). James Beasley and William Kendal, overseers assigned to these roads, and William Bell owned land around Swift Run in "Greene" County (May 1763 p. 84, *OCDB* 13:279), and Francis Conway patented 5000 acres on the Conway River in southern "Madison" County (*VPB* 14:450).

Five years later, William Lucas was granted his petition for "a Road to Turn out of the Main Road about a mile above the new Church and to Come in about a mile Below" (**27 October 1768,**

27 April 1769). This is the first mention in the Orange County road orders of a "New Church" since the "New (Upper) Church" on **27 May 1742**[A].[1] William Lucas had served on roads to the Upper Church from 1743 to 1763;[2] but after 1768, he only worked on roads to this "New Church," which was much closer to his residence on Welshman Run, about a mile west of Ruckersville in "Greene" County.[3] Others assigned to work on this road "above the new Church" also owned land in "Greene" County.[4]

The only known colonial church in "Greene" County was a church near Ruckersville called, in the nineteenth century, the Orange Church. The "Chappel" and "New Church" in the 1760s road orders must be this Orange Church, and it must have been one of the four—with the Middle, Upper, and Pine Stake—churches referred to in a 4 February 1762 letter written by Rev. James Marye, Jr., minister of St. Thomas' Parish, requesting "four small collections [of books] to be sent as lending libraries at his four churches."[5] This "New Church"—the last Anglican church built in St. Thomas' Parish—is only called the "New Church" or the "Church" in the road orders. The name "Orange Church" or "church near Ruckersville" seem to have been post-colonial names. Here, it will be called the New (Orange) Church.

On **26 April 1770** and **28 June 1770**, a road was petitioned and granted "from Boxen Camp into the Road that leads Down to the new Church." This Boxing Camp was probably just that, a place where boxing took place. Boxing was a popular sport among the English aristocracy in the eighteenth century.[6] It also appears to have been popular in Orange County, according to a letter written by Governor William Gooch in 1735 to the Bishop of London complaining about the behavior of Rev. John Beckett, minister of St. Mark's Parish from 1733 to 1740: "Mr. Beckett is a man of strong constitution, loves drink perhaps too well, and living in the Northern Neck where drinking and boxing is too much in fashion, has been tempted to quarrel."[7]

The location of the Boxing Camp is not known. It is mentioned in sixteen road orders between 1750 and 1790, usually in descriptions of the major west-east road from Swift Run Gap to the Mountain Road ending at Fredericksburg (Routes 33, 609, 20). The western section of this road was described as the road from Swift Run Gap to Boxing Camp to the Red Oak Level (26 July 1750 p. 7), Swift Run Gap crossing the Blue Run to the Boxing Camp (24 July 1755 p. 39) and the foot of Powell's Mountain to Boxing Camp to the Red Oak Level (28 May 1761 p. 74). These descriptions place Boxing Camp about midway between Swift Run Gap and the Red Oak Level (see pp. 31–32) and east of where Blue Run crosses Route 33 near Stanardsville, which was, as suggested by David Covey, possibly near the intersection of Routes 33 and 609.[8]

After 1774, there are several orders for work on a Church Road near the New (Orange) Church: "the Church Road about a Quarter of a Mile below the Church" (**27 October 1774[B], 26 May 1780**), "swift run down to the Church road" (**23 December 1784, 26 October 1790[F], 23 April 1793[G&H]**),[9] "Burtons Mill from thence to the Church road" (**24 September 1787, 27 February 1797**) and "Connallys New Building On the Church Road" (**25 September 1797[B]**). All these orders describe places and householders in the vicinity of the New (Orange) Church, and this Church Road may be the "Road to Turn out of the Main Road about a mile above the new Church and to Come in about a mile Below" ordered cleared on **27 October 1768**.

This Church Road was one of several church and chapel roads in greater Orange County. There was a Chapel Road to the Southwest Mountain Chapel (**18 February 1734/35[C]**), a New Church Road to the Upper Church (**24 January 1744/45, 27 June 1745, 22 August 1745**), a Pine Stake Church Road (*OCDB* 19:427 and, possibly, **24 May 1759**) and a Church Road probably to the Middle Church (**27 May 1756, 27 July 1769**). (Contemporary maps call Route 631 the "Brick Church Road" or the "Church Run Road.")

An interesting Orange County deed, dated 25 April 1791, described a piece of land, which had been given for the construction of the "Upper Church." However, examination of this deed leaves no doubt that the land given was for the New

(Orange) Church and not the Upper Church.

> I Jeremiah White of County of Orange . . . have
> given unto Richard White of County of Orange . . .
> for the love I have unto my son Richard White 209
> acres of land in County of Orange, being land
> Jeremiah White bought of Joshua Stapp and
> bounded Beginning at two small pines close by the
> Road on the West side thence North to two pines on
> the old line thence South to a Chesnut in a thicket by
> the Edge of the old field; thence North to the
> Beginning together with its appurtenances whatsover
> to the same belonging Except Eleven acres of which
> four acres formerly given to please the Upper
> Church in St. Thomas Parish on: and Seven acres
> Joining the said Church line in the Corner which
> belongeth by a former Contract to William Lucas . . .
> (*OCDB* 20:6).

The location of this 209 acres is revealed by tracing back transfers of this and adjoining properties. On 19 September 1787, Joshua Stapp, Jr. sold Jeremiah White 209 acres in Orange County: "land which Joshua Stapps Father bought of Mr. John Walden of Caroline County" and later gave to his son, Joshua Stapp, Jr. on 28 March 1771 (*OCDB* 19:173). The 28 March 1771 deed contains almost the same description of the 209 acres as the 1791 deed: "eleven acres of which four acres given to place [not "please"] the upper church in Saint Thomas's Parish on . . . and seven acres joining the said Church line in the corner which belongeth to Mr. Wm. Lucas" (*OCDB* 15:306). On 31 March 1772, Joshua Stapp, Sr. sold Thomas Burbage "200 acres, part of Brooksby Tract and part of the land Stap purchased of Mr. John Walden of Caroline County . . . bounded Joshua Stap Junr" (*OCDB* 15:465). This deed, describing land adjoining the 209 acres with four acres "to place the upper church," identifies some or all of these two parcels of land as originally part of George Braxton's Brookesby Tract. (Joshua Stapp, Sr.'s deed of purchase from John Walden—and with it, the date of the transaction—was not found.)

The "Upper Church" mentioned in these deeds cannot be the Upper Church in northwest "Orange" County because the Brookesby Tract—10,000 acres patented to George Braxton and others in 1722 (*VPB* 14:399)—was in southeast "Greene" County; because Stapp's 209 acres adjoined William Lucas' land in eastern "Greene" County close to the New (Orange) Church and the Church Road;[10] and because the Upper Church was on Robert Beverley's Octonia Grant and no part of this grant was ever part of the Brookesby Tract or bequeathed or sold to a John Walden.[11]

There are two possible explanations for the New (Orange) Church being called the Upper Church in these deeds. One explanation, seen occasionally in the road orders and the St. Mark's parish vestry orders, is a simple case of miswriting the name of one church when another was meant.[12] Another possibility is that when Stapp's 1771 deed was written—at least ten years after the construction of the New (Orange) Church and probably at a time when the thirty-year-old Upper Church was being called the Old Church[13]—the New (Orange) Church, now the most western of the parish churches, was considered to be an "upper" church.

Finally, a curious order appears on **26 June 1797**: "John White appointed overseer of the road from the new Church to Abraham Howsworths & ordered that the hands that workd under William Lucas S^r. Clear the s^d Precincts." What was this "new Church"? William Lucas and John White worked on many roads to the New (Orange) Church; but why would a thirty-six-year-old church, which had not been called the "New Church" since **27 April 1770**, now be called new? It seems highly unlikely that the Anglicans built a new church in 1797, since between 1778 and 1784 the Virginia Assembly passed several acts disestablishing the Anglican church and leaving parish vestries without the financial resources of the annual tithe. Were meetinghouses now called churches? Did the Anglican parishioners fund the rebuilding of the New (Orange) Church? Or, should the order have read *the new Church Road*?

The New (Orange) Church, built ca. 1761 near today's Ruckersville

in Greene County, may have survived longer than any of the
other colonial churches in St. Thomas' Parish, but documented
evidence detailing what happened to it in the nineteenth century
is still needed. Rev. Joseph Earnest remarked in 1857 that the
"Orange Church . . . near Ruckersville . . . is still standing, though it
has long ceased to be used as a place of worship by an Episcopal
congregation. . . . The old church, which is of wood, has under-
gone so many repairs since the time it was built, that it is
thought, like the old frigate Constitution, little if any of the
original timber is to be found in it." And, "Mr. Richard White,
who died some years since [1841] at the age of ninety, was the
last communicate connected with the Old Orange Church."[14]
According to the Ruckersville Church website, "The history of
the Ruckersville Baptist Church is traced back to the old Orange
Church . . . located ½ mile from Ruckersville. . . . On the 9th of
June 1879, the church was moved to Ruckersville and called the
Union Church. In 1892 the Baptist Congregation organized and
worshipped here until 1908, at which time the present church
was erected."[15]

THE MINISTERS
OF COLONIAL ST. THOMAS' PARISH

This brief description of the ministers, who served the parishioners of St. Thomas' Parish from 1721—when the parish was still part of St. George's Parish—to 1800, includes some corrections and additions to earlier published accounts about these ministers. This is not a definitive examination of the subject; more work is needed in future.

Reverend Theodosius Staige, 1726–1729. The first minister known to have been hired by the St. George's vestry was the Reverend Theodosius Staige. He was appointed and took up residence in Germanna in 1726, a year after he arrived in Virginia.[1] According to Paula Felder, Staige "had a stressful amount of territory to cover," and by 1728, he was not on cordial terms with the vestry and left the parish in 1728 or 1729. Staige was then appointed minister of Charles Parish, York County, Virginia, where he served—again with complaints leveled against him by the vestry—until his death on 26 December 1747.[2]

Reverend Rodham Kenner, 1729–1731. On 11 March 1728/29, the St. George's vestry interviewed the Reverends Lawrence DeButts and Rodham Kenner for the position of parish minister. They offered Kenner the position, and he resided at Germanna until the glebe house, on the Po River, was completed. Shortly after Kenner was hired by the St. George's vestry, he married Judith Beverley, daughter of prominent landlord and St. George's vestryman, Harry Beverley, in Spotsylvania County on 1 June 1729. Kenner was serving St. George's Parish when St. Mark's Parish was formed in 1731. On 10 April 1731, he was discharged from his position but continued to serve St. George's as a supply minister from 7 February 1731/32 until 9 January 1732/33 when the vestry hired the Reverend Patrick Henry (*StGVB*, 9–30). Rodham Kenner's estate was settled June 1737 in Caroline County, Virginia.[3]

Reverends Lawrence DeButts and Francis Peart, 1731–1733.
From 1 January 1731 until May 1733, as Philip Slaughter engagingly put it, "St. Mark's Parish now begins its independent career at Germanna, without a shepherd to seek after the flock scattered in the wilderness bounded by the Blue Mountains. . . . For the several years in which they had no pastor the vestry employed occasionally the Rev. Mr. De Butts and the Rev. Mr. Purit, two adventurers who were seeking parishes, and paid them three hundred pounds of tobacco per sermon." To supplement these paid-by-the-sermon ministers, "the churches and chapels were served by Lay readers, or clerks, as they were then called, whom the vestries seem to have preferred to inefficient clergymen."[4]

The Reverend Lawrence DeButts (also De Butts, Debutts, de Butts) was paid passage from England to Virginia in 1721. Upon arrival in Virginia, he was appointed to Washington Parish, Westmoreland County, and later served St. Stephen's Parish in Northumberland County, Farnham Parish in Richmond County, and Cople Parish in Westmoreland County. On 7 February 1728/29, St. George's vestry rejected his application for parish minister in favor of Rev. Rodham Kenner. But DeButts did serve as a supply minister, since the 29 September 1731 vestry minutes note his complaint about nonpayment for seven sermons (*StGVB*, 8, 9, 20). Between 8 October 1731 and 9 October 1733, the St. Mark's vestry paid DeButts for delivering fifty-four sermons as a supply minister (*StMVB*, 9, 13, 52). In 1735, he was appointed minister of William and Mary Parish, St. Mary's County, Maryland, where he remained until his death in 1752.[5]

The Reverend Francis Peart was paid passage from England to minister in Virginia on 11 December 1730. Francis Peart was the minister of St. Stephen's Parish, Northumberland County, from 1731 to 1742.[6] But on 29 September 1731, the St. George's vestry paid him for preaching eleven sermons (*StGVB*, 21); on 8 October 1731, the St. Mark's vestry paid him for preaching at Germanna (*StMVB*, 9), and on 2 October 1733, the St. George's vestry again paid him "for Coming part of his way three times to preach in this parish" (*StGVB*, 34). Francis Peart, then, was not, as characterized by Slaughter, an adventurer seeking a parish, but a minister of another parish, who offered his services to two parishes temporarily without ministers.

Reverend John Becket, 1733–1740. On 11 May 1733, the St. Mark's vestry "ordered that the Reverend Mr. John Becket being Recommended to us by the Governour and Commissary we doe Entertain him as Minister of our parish and that he . . . doe receive the Gleeb Land and what is up on it this day and the house when finished he haveing thereunto agreed" (*StMVB*, 13). The Reverend John Becket had sailed from England in 1727 and upon arrival in Virginia, was appointed to minister in St. James Northam Parish, Goochland County.[7]

Dissatisfaction with Becket, the first minister of St. Mark's Parish, was expressed two years later in 1735, when Governor William Gooch wrote the Bishop of London to complain about Mr. Becket's inappropriate behavior: "Mr. Beckett is a man of strong constitution, loves drink perhaps too well, and living in the Northern Neck where drinking and boxing is too much in fashion, has been tempted to quarrel."[8] Then, on 10 October 1735, the vestry reminded Becket of his duties when it ordered him to "preach at every Church and Chapel in Saint Mark Parish according as the Law Directs;" in 1737, the Orange County court fined him for over-charging a marriage fee and concealing a tithable;[9] and on 13 June 1739, the vestry ordered the church wardens to "take all Evidence to prove all the allegations presented to his Excellentcy the Governour and Commissary against the Reverend Mr. John Becket." Six months later, on 7 January 1739/40, the vestry ordered "that the Church wardens agree with the Reverend Mr. MacDaniel if he please to serve the parish for their present suply and if not some other Minister Except Mr. Becket." On 4 April 1741, the vestry closed their account with Becket (*StMVB*, 19, 24, 26, 29). But John Becket, who had acquired 400 acres on Riga Run in 1735 (*OCDB* 2:67), remained in the county and would later seek appointment as minister of St. Thomas' Parish.

Reverend -?- MacDaniel, 1740(?). Apparently the Reverend Mr.

MacDaniel accepted the 7 January 1740 St. Mark's vestry offer to serve as their supply minister, because he was paid for six sermons delivered in 1740. However, on 10 June 1740, the St. Mark's vestry hired the Reverend John Thompson to be the parish minister, and after that date, there is no further mention of MacDaniel in the St. Mark's vestry book (*StMVB*, 26, 27).

But did MacDaniel serve St. Thomas' Parish when it was formed at the end of 1740? Is he the "old Scotch minister of the Episcopal Church" Joseph Earnest referred to when he wrote, "in 1740,—the year in which St. Thomas was formed into a separate parish . . . an old Scotch minister of the Episcopal Church, whose name I have not been able to ascertain, but who it seems was fond of good cheer and a game of cards, officiated regularly at this church. He resided with Mr. Benjamin Cave, Sen., a first settler, whose residence was but a short distance from where the old church stood."[10] Philip Slaughter also referred to "one of the old ministers, about 1740, [who] lived with Benjamin Cave, Sr." But Slaughter added that this minister, "whom Mr. Ernest could not identify, was either De Butts or Becket".[11]

This "old Scotch minister" could not have been Lawrence DeButts because he was in Maryland in 1740, but there are four other possible candidates. The first possibility is Rev. MacDaniel. A Reverend Daniel McDonald was paid passage from England to minister in Virginia in 1731.[12] Since the surnames MacDaniel and MacDonald are often confused,[13] it is possible that this Rev. Daniel McDonald—about whom little is known--was the Mr. MacDaniel who served as a supply minister in St. Mark's Parish in 1740 and was the "old Scotch minister" Ernest identified as the first minister of St. Thomas' Parish. The second possibility is the Reverend Robert Rose, a young Scot (see below), who appeared in Orange County documents from 1738. The third possibility is Rev. John Becket. Although his surname is not Scottish, he was still living in the area in 1740, was trying to gain appointment to St. Thomas' Parish (see below) and Gov. Gooch's complaint about him, noted above, does describe a man "fond of good cheer." Finally, and most likely, it may have been the Reverend Richard Hartswell, who Ulysses P. Joyner, Jr. and

William H. B. Thomas identified as the first minister of St. Thomas' Parish.[14] Although Hartswell is not a Scottish name, documents—presented below—reveal him to have been "fond of good cheer" like Earnest's "old Scotch minister." The identity of the first minister of St. Thomas' Parish was probably recorded in the parish's vestry minutes, which detailed the appointments and tenure of all ministers and supply ministers engaged by the vestry. But these vestry records are lost, and, in their absence, other documents must be used to reconstruct this information.

Reverends Richard Hartswell and Robert Rose, ca. 1740–ca. 1750. A poem penned by a "Rev. Mr. Hartswell" during his voyage to Virginia was printed in the *Virginia Gazette* on 1 February 1739/40, and a "Rev. Richard Hartswell" was also reported in the same newspaper, on 4 January 1739/40, to have attended a man condemned to hanging in Williamsburg.[15] In 1740, "an agreement was made with a Rev. Mr. Hartwell to become the minister [in Bristol Parish, Prince George County]; but, misunderstandings taking place as to the terms, it was never carried into execution."[16] The next report of Hartswell is in November 1741 when the Orange County court leveled charges against the parish minister for drunkenness. Although the charges were dropped, he was said to have left the parish in disgrace. Then, on 11 April 1743, Rev. Richard Hartswell was fined for drunkenness and swearing by the neighboring Louisa County court.[17] Hartswell probably arrived in Virginia in late 1739 and was appointed minister of St. Thomas' Parish sometime between 1740 and November 1741. How long before he vacated his post after the accusations of insobriety is not known, but a Richard Hartswell—an uncommon name—appeared as a witness on two Orange County deeds in 1744 (*OCDB* 9:141).

It is not known who served the parishioners of St. Thomas' Parish in the years between Richard Hartswell's court appearances—and possible dismissal—and the appointment of the Reverend Mungo Marshall in the late 1740s–early 1750s. William H. B. Thomas described in some detail the futile byzantine attempts by Rev. John Becket to gain the position of minister of the parish in 1745 in place of the "present minister, a 'jobber' they call him, [who] comes only on weekends."[18] Who was this "jobber" (did Becket mean a supply minister or a man using his appointment for private gain?) serving the parish in 1745? Was it still Richard Hartswell, or could it have been the Reverend Robert Rose? Robert Rose, a highly respected clergyman and diarist, was born 1704 in Scotland and was paid passage to minister in Virginia in 1726. He appeared in Orange County documents as early as 1738, was executor of Alexander Spotswood's estate in the 1740s and was appointed minister of St. Anne's Parish, Albemarle County, in 1745 or 1746.[19]

Reverend Mungo Marshall, ca. 1750–1757. Joseph Earnest wrote, "In 1753, the name of the Rev. Mungo Marshall appears for the first time in connection with this [St. Thomas] parish, though it is probable he took charge of the same at an earlier period. He continued to reside here until the time of his death, which took place either in 1757 or 1758. . . . He was buried in the churchyard attached to the Old Brick Church." Philip Slaughter said Rev. Mungo Marshall was minister of St. Thomas' Parish from 1753 to 1760, and W. W. Scott dated his tenure 1753–1758.[20]

The Reverend Mungo Marshall, another Scot, arrived in Virginia 1744 or 1745. He is documented in Orange County as early as 1746 (*OCDB* 10:338); on 16 March 1747, he married Lucy Marye, daughter of Rev. James Marye, Sr., the highly respected minister of St. George's Parish; in 1749, the "tithables of Rev. Mungo Marshal" were ordered to do some road work (24 November 1749 p. 142); and on **26 July 1750**, he petitioned for a road to be cleared from the Glebe, the minister's residence.[21] Whether Marshall was appointed minister of St. Thomas' Parish as early as 1746, the two road orders confirm his appointment to the parish to no later than 1749 or 1750.

Later documents record Marshall baptizing two children of James Madison, Sr. in 1753 and 1756 and writing to the Associates of Dr. Thomas Bray for Founding Clerical Libraries and Supporting Negro Schools on 15 December 1756, "desiring books and tracts to help in instructing the Negroes."[22] Mungo Marshall's will was recorded in Orange County on 25 May 1757 (*OCWB* 2:266).

The Years 1757–1760. Philip Slaughter and Joseph Earnest said the Reverend William Giberne succeeded Mungo Marshall in 1760. Earnest said "his residence here was a brief one; (he removed to Richmond County, Virginia) for at the close of the year 1761, the Rev. James Marye, Jr., . . . commenced his ministry in Orange." However, documents do not support Giberne's appointment—however brief—as minister of St. Thomas' Parish. On 22 February 1758, apparently in the absence of a regular minister in St. Thomas' Parish, Rev. James Marye, Sr., minister of St. George's Parish, Spotsylvania County, baptized Catlett Madison, son of James Madison, Sr.; and on 6 March 1760, William Giberne baptized Madison's daughter, Nelly, in St. Thomas' Parish. However, in letters written by Rev. James Marye, Jr. on 2 August 1760 and 1 October 1761, Marye stated that he had succeeded the late Rev. Mungo Marshall.[23]

Slaughter and Earnest probably assumed Giberne succeeded Marshall because he baptized Nelly Madison in 1760. However, it is likely that during this short period when St. Thomas was without a minister, James Madison, Sr. called on Giberne, who was "generally considered to be the most popular preacher in the colony," to perform the baptism of his child, just as he had called on James Marye, Sr. of neighboring St. George's Parish, to perform the same duty in 1758. Giberne was minister of Hanover Parish, King George County, in 1759 and Lunenburg Parish, Richmond County, from 1762 to 1795.[24]

Reverend James Marye, Jr., 1760–1768. The Reverend James Marye, Jr. (also spelled Mayre, Maury, Marie, Mary) was appointed minister of St. Thomas' Parish sometime between 6 March 1760 when William Giberne baptized Nelly Madison and 2 August 1760 when Marye, Jr. wrote that he had succeeded Mungo Marshall. James Marye, Jr., son of Rev. James Marye, Sr., minister of St. George's Parish, was born 1731 in Virginia and educated at William and Mary. In 1755, he was ordained in England, as required by the Anglican Church in order to qualify to minister in his homeland. He served St. Thomas' Parish until

1768 when he succeeded his father as minister of St. George's Parish, Spotsylvania County.[25] Joseph Earnest praised the younger Marye as "a worthy exception to a class of clergy that obtained in Virginia in olden time. So far as we can learn, he was a man of evangelical views and sincere piety."[26] This high opinion seems borne out by a number of letters Marye wrote between 1760 and 1765 to the Associates of Dr. Thomas Bray for the Founding of Clerical Libraries and Supporting Negro Schools concerning his efforts to build a school for and educate the "young Negroes" of his parish; to educate the orphaned sons of his predecessor, Mungo Marshall; and his plans to build a library and stock it with books "especialy against Swearing & gaming."[27]

Reverend Thomas Martin, 1768–1770. The Reverend Thomas Martin succeeded James Marye, Jr. in 1768 (he baptized Elizabeth Madison on 22 February 1768). But Martin's tenure was cut short by his death in September 1770. Thomas Martin was born 1743 in New Jersey, educated at Princeton and ordained in England in 1767. His intellectual accomplishments were highly regarded, and he was hired by James Madison, Sr. to tutor his children, including the future president of the United States, James Madison, Jr.[28]

Reverend John Barnett, 1771–1772. Philip Slaughter and Joseph Earnest said the Reverend John Barnett succeeded Thomas Martin. Earnest, probably referring to Barnett's baptism of Reuben Madison on 10 November 1771, said, "His name occurs officially in 1771. But his connection with the parish was also of brief duration, for in 1774 the Rev. John Wingate was the minister."[29] Two advertisements in the *Virginia Gazette* on 19 and 26 March 1772, which gave notice "that the Parish of St. Thomas, in Orange County, is become vacant by the resignation of Mr. John ["Thomas" in 19 March version] Barnett, the late Incumbant," date Barnett's tenure as minister of St. Thomas' Parish from 1771 to early 1772.[30]

Reverend John Wingate, ca. 1772–ca. 1777. The Reverend John Wingate was appointed minister of St. Thomas' Parish sometime between 1772 when the parish advertised for a minister and 30 October 1774 when he baptized Frances, daughter of James Madison, Sr. He served the parish until at least 25 February 1777 when he performed the marriage of Thomas Foster.[31] But his later years in the parish must not have been comfortable. On 15 April 1775, the Orange Committee for Safety reported in the *Virginia Gazette* that Rev. John Wingate had in his possession "several pamphlets, containing very obnoxious reflections on the Continental Congress." When the Committee requested, "in the most respectful manner," that Wingate hand over these pamphlets, he resisted, arguing that they were not his to release. Eventually, under protest, he gave them up and the pamphlets were promptly burned at a public gathering. The report concluded that the citizens of Orange "joined in expressing a noble indignation against such execrable publications, and their ardent wishes for an opportunity of inflicting on the authors, publishers and their abettors, the punishment due to their insufferable arrogance, and atrocious crimes."[32] Wingate eventually took up the rectorship of St. George's Parish on the island of Grenada and died there in 1789.[33]

The Years 1778–1800. Between 1778 and 1784, the Virginia Assembly, reflecting general dissatisfaction with the power, financial burden and excesses of the Anglican church, suspended the salaries of clergymen, removed the church's right to collect taxes and disestablished the Anglican church as the state church of Virginia. The consequences of these laws can be seen in two entries in the St. Mark's vestry book: in 1777 it was "Ordered, that the churchwardens advertise the vacancy of this parish and the renting of the glebe," and in 1778 "The General Assembly having suspended the salaries of clergymen, the vestry met to fix on some method of paying the salaries of the officers of the church."[34] On 26 December 1785, the Virginia General Assembly adopted Thomas Jefferson's Statute of Religious Freedom, which guaranteed Virginians the freedom "to profess, and by argument maintain, their opinions in matters of religion."[35] The final chapter of the Anglican church in Virginia came in 1800 when the Virginia Assembly passed an act confiscating all the properties of the church. The result of this act can be seen in the fate of the Middle (Brick) Church, which, in about 1806, was "torn down, brick by brick, and its bricks used for chimneys, walks, etc., and its graveyard was robbed of its tombstones, which were used as lintels, etc., so that today there is nothing to denote its location, or that of its sleeping population, except a few scattered bricks that mark the site of the old building."[36]

During this period, Philip Slaughter said the St. Thomas' Parish vestry appointed no minister to serve the parish because "The disloyal odor [Rev. John Wingate] left behind him" caused the patriotic members of the vestry to eschew another minister who might express allegiance to the crown.[37] Lay readers and supply ministers were paid to answer the needs of the parish: the Reverend Matthew (Marye) Maury of Albemarle County; the Reverend Alexander Belmaine; Henry Frye, a Methodist; James Waddell, "the blind Presbyterian Minster," who preached for two years at the Middle (Brick) Church; and the Reverend Charles O'Neill, who was appointed minister of St. Thomas' Parish in the 1790s and served until 1800.[38]

THE HISTORIANS
OF COLONIAL ST. THOMAS' PARISH

The first known history of colonial St. Thomas' Parish is Bishop William Meade's *Old Churches, Ministers, and Families of Virginia*, published in 1857. Meade explained in his preface that his work relied on documents dating back to 1632 and on the contributions made by numerous friends. In "St. Mark's Parish, Culpeper County," he quoted several passages from the St. Mark's vestry book about the Germanna Church, he noted that the "(Southwest) Mountain Chapel" existed before the formation of St. Mark's Parish, and he drew attention to the vestry's order to build the "(Southwest) Mountain Church." However, Meade made no suggestions about the locations and histories of the Southwest Mountain Chapel and Church.[1]

In his introduction to "Orange County – St. Thomas Parish," Meade explained that this article was quoted from the "pen and labours" of Rev. Joseph Earnest. (The Reverend Joseph Earnest was minister of St. Thomas' Parish from 1840 to 1866.)[2] Earnest's contribution was anecdotal: his article relied on his observations and local traditions. Whether he was unaware of the St. Mark's vestry book or chose to ignore it, he did not mention, by name, the Southwest Mountain Chapel or Church. He called the earliest house of worship in St. Thomas' Parish the "church in the wilderness" or the "first 'Orange Church' " and said, "The first church that was built in the parish was situated about ten miles northwest of Orange Court-House, on a portion of land now owned by Mr. Robert Brooking. . . . a short distance from this 'church in the wilderness,' upon the right bank of the Rapidan River, is yet to be seen an ancient mound, or burial-place of the Indians." (In the mid-nineteenth century, the Brooking family owned several properties near the "ancient [Indian] mound," about one mile east of the Greene County line near the Rapidan.)[3] Benjamin Cave, a former St. Mark's vestryman, lived "a short distance from where the old church stood. . . . At what period of time this first 'Orange Church' was built, we have it not in our power exactly to verify. We have been told that it was frequented as a place of worship by some of the old settlers as early as 1723. Certain it is, that it was used as such in 1740,—the year in which St. Thomas was formed into a separate parish. . . . Subsequently, as the settlements advanced westward, the old church was removed about eight miles distant to the place where its remains [i.e., his "Orange Church" near Ruckersville] are still standing."[4]

Earnest made no connection between his "first church that was built in the parish" and the Southwest Mountain Chapel or the Southwest Mountain Church. He said the "Orange Church" near Ruckersville, which replaced the "first church that was built in the parish" was the second oldest church in St. Thomas' Parish. He did not say when the one church replaced the other, but he implied it was after 1740, since he said the first church was still being used in 1740.[5]

Philip Slaughter wrote in the preface of his *A History of St. Mark's Parish, Culpeper County, Virginia, with Notes of Old Churches and Old Families and Illustrations of the Manners and Customs of the Olden Time*, published 1877, that he believed "he was the first person who conceived the idea of writing a history of the old parishes in Virginia upon the basis of the old vestry-books and registers." His first work, *History of St. George's Parish, in Spotsylvania and diocese of Virginia*, appeared in 1847; but illness forced him to suspend his research, and "Bishop Meade, the most competent of all men for this special task, was induced to take up the subject, and the result was the valuable work, 'The Old Churches and Families of Virginia,' in which the author's histories of St. George and Bristol Parishes, and some other materials which he had gathered, were incorporated. The author, [Slaughter] in his old age, returns to his first love, and submits to the public a history of his native parish of St. Mark's."[6]

Slaughter relied on the St. Mark's vestry book and Joseph Earnest's article for his identification of the early churches and chapels in St. Thomas' Parish; his descriptions of these houses of worship appear in three sections of his book: on St. Mark's

Parish, St. Thomas' Parish and a short sketch of the Cave Family.[7]

Referring to the St. Mark's vestry minutes, Slaughter correctly identified the Germanna Church, the Southwest Mountain Chapel, the Southwest Mountain Church and the chapel at Battaley's Quarter as the two chapels and two churches existing in St. Thomas' Parish before its formation in 1740. He also correctly noted that the vestry assigned William Phillips and David Cave to read at the Southwest Mountain Chapel and David Cave to read at the Southwest Mountain Church (which he called the "old Orange Church"). However, Slaughter's other observations about St. Thomas' churches and chapels are confusing and sometimes contradictory. In one place, Slaughter said the Southwest Mountain Chapel was built "not far from Cave's Ford in Orange;" but in another place, he repeated Earnest when he said this "first chapel" was "near Brooking" and Benjamin Cave, Sr.'s eighteenth-century residence. He said the Southwest Mountain Church—which he consistently called the "old Orange Church near Ruckersville"—was built near Ruckersville; but in another place he followed Earnest when he implied it was first built in northwest Orange County and later moved to near Ruckersville. Slaughter also said, in his section on St. Thomas' Parish, that the St. Mark's vestry built three—not two—houses of worship in what would become St. Thomas' Parish: the "old Orange church, near Ruckersville;" the chapel at Battaley's Quarter; and a third house of worship, the "chapel where Robert Brooken now lives," which he earlier described as the first chapel in St. Thomas' Parish, i.e. the Southwest Mountain Chapel.

In *A History of Orange County, Virginia*, 1907, W. W. Scott said the second oldest church in Orange County, after the Germanna Church, "was in the Brooking neighborhood near (old) Cave's ford, about three miles northwest of Somerset, and was later removed to the vicinity of Ruckersville."[8] Scott disagreed with the dates Earnest (1723) and Slaughter (before 1740) assigned to this chapel near Brooking's; he suggested it was "most probably . . . built about 1740 when St. Thomas Parish was cut off from St.

Mark."[9] It is interesting that, although Scott subscribed to Earnest's and Slaughter's identification of St. Thomas' oldest churches, he dated—without any explanation—the church "in the Brooking neighborhood" to shortly after the formation of St. Thomas' Parish, i.e., the date suggested here for the Upper Church, which stood in the vicinity of this "Brooking neighborhood."

The first work which used county court records to shed light on the parish churches was *St. Thomas Parish, Orange County, Virginia,* written ca. 1931 by J. William Browning, County Clerk of Orange County from 1919 to 1936. Browning said the "Upper Church was situated near 'Old Cave's Ford' [on the Rapidan River]" and was the oldest of the three early churches (with the Middle and Pine Stake Churches) in St. Thomas' Parish. If Browning meant the Upper Church was the first house of worship built by the St. Thomas' vestry, he was correct (he offered no date of construction). And if his location of the Upper Church "near Old Cave's Ford" was meant to be Scott's "in the Brooking neighborhood near (old) Cave's ford, about three miles northwest of Somerset," then Browning was the first to correctly identify the name of the house of worship which stood in this area.[10]

In *'Faith of our Fathers! . . .' Religion and the Churches in Colonial Orange County,* a 1975 Bicentennial paper, William H. B. Thomas agreed with Joseph Earnest, Philip Slaughter and W. W. Scott that the [Southwest] Mountain Chapel (Earnest and Scott did not call it this) was in northwest "Orange" County "some few miles northwest of Somerset and not far from the Rapidan River," and that the new church the St. Mark's vestry ordered built below the Southwest Mountain Chapel in 1733—which he called the Orange Church, not the Southwest Mountain Church—was later moved to near Ruckersville. But Thomas submitted that the chapel which was ordered built by the St. Mark's vestry in 1733 near Battaley's Quarter (the Upper Chapel) "was erected in the same vicinity [northwest of Somerset, near the Rapidan], perhaps taking the place of the Mountain Chapel."[11]

J. Randolph Grymes, Jr., in his 1977 work *The Octonia Grant*, also said the Southwest Mountain Chapel was in northwest Orange County (on the Octonia Grant). He did not suggest a date for the chapel, and his location "near Church Run and also near the Mountain Road" simply used different landmarks to describe the same location suggested earlier.[12]

Ulysses P. Joyner, Jr., in his 1987 work, *The First Settlers of Orange County, Virginia 1700–1776*, identified the Germanna Church and the "[Southwest] Mountain Chapel" as the oldest houses of worship in St. Thomas' Parish. He said, "There is some dispute as to the location of the Mountain Chapel, but there is evidence that it existed as early as 1723." (This date was suggested by Earnest, but his only "evidence" was local tradition.) Joyner said, "the Mountain Chapel was located just west of the present Town of Orange near Cave's Ford." But in the 1780s, during the period of the dissolution of the Anglican church, "the 'Mountain Chapel' moved from its location near Montford [Montford is near Cave's Ford] further up the Rapidan . . . to a point near the Indian Mound and if it still exists, is used as a farm storage barn." He expanded on this when he added, "there is a small building today (1985) located on the Colvin property near the Indian Mound [where previous historians had placed the Southwest Mountain Chapel or "first church" in St. Thomas' Parish], which may well be the remains of the Mountain Chapel according to historian William H. B. Thomas."[13]

It is curious that Joyner did not mention the Southwest Mountain Church; that he offered no evidence for placing the Southwest Mountain Chapel near Cave's Ford (as had been suggested earlier by Slaughter and Scott); and that he said—without supporting evidence—the Mountain Chapel was moved five miles west from Cave's Ford (Montford) to near the Indian Mound and later became (when?) a storage barn.[14]

Joyner came close to recognizing the connection between the Southwest Mountain Chapel, Southwest Mountain Church and the Middle (Brick) Church when he suggested that Rev. Theodosius

Staige, the first minister of St. George's Parish, was instrumental in building the Middle Church before 1729 (see here pp. 12, 34–36).

Finally, Ann L. Miller took a fresh look at this subject in her chapter "Early German and Anglican Churches of Culpeper County, 1714–1865" in *Early Churches of Culpeper County, Virginia: Colonial and Ante-Bellum Congregations*, ca. 1987. She noted four houses of worship in St. Thomas' Parish predating its formation in 1740: the Germanna Church, the (Southwest) Mountain Chapel, the Southwest Mountain Church and the Upper Chapel.

Miller said the 16 June 1729 entry in the St. George's vestry book[15] identified the "Mountain Chapel" as the second oldest house of worship in St. Thomas' Parish. She placed it "near the Rapidan River in what is today southern Madison or western Orange County" based on the 11 December 1733 St. Mark's vestry order to build the Southwest Mountain Church "with in a Mile of the first run below the [Mountain] Chapel" (*StMVB*, 15) and a 10 October 1737 vestry order for "the Clk. of the vestry [to] deliver unto David Kinked on his Security the bond and articles relating to the building the Mountain Church upon Mr. Barbers as sum set to glase the windows of the said church (*StMVB*, 22)." Miller interpreted this 1737 order to mean that the Mountain Church, which she correctly said replaced the Mountain Chapel, was on James Barbour's property, which "lay on the north bank of the Rapidan River in what is now Madison County. . . . on Rt. 231 north of the Rapidan River." But since the evidence presented above clearly places the Southwest Mountain Chapel and Southwest Mountain Church where the later Middle Church stood, the reading of the "upon" in this order should not be read as a location, but as *upon the sum set by Mr. Barbour (a St. Mark's vestryman) to glaze the windows*. Miller also identified the chapel, which the vestry ordered Benjamin Cave to find a site for near Mosley Battaley's Quarter, as the Upper Chapel, but she did not suggest a location for it.[16]

In Antebellum Orange: The Pre-Civil War Homes, Public Buildings and Historic Sites of Orange County, Virginia, 1988, Ann Miller noted "a small building now used as a granary" north of the Carolton house in the northwest corner of the county, which "local tradition credits . . . with having been an early church; both the early Anglican 'Mountain Chapel' of the 1720's and a late 18th century chapel, probably used by a Baptist congregation, are known to have stood in the vicinity, and this little building may have been one of these."[17] With Miller's acceptance of this "local tradition," which Joyner attributed to William H. B. Thomas, she narrowed her earlier suggested location for the (Southwest) Mountain Chapel from "southern Madison or western Orange" to northwest Orange County.

These historians agreed—with minor differences of a few miles here and a few decades there—about the locations and histories of the Germanna, Middle and Pine Stake Churches.[18] But the Southwest Mountain Chapel, Southwest Mountain Church, Upper Chapel, Upper Church and New (Orange) Church were— if even mentioned—mired in confusion.

Philip Slaughter and Ann Miller, quoting the 11 December 1733 St. Mark's vestry order, made passing references to the Upper Chapel; and William H. B. Thomas suggested it was built near Somerset. Hints in the St. Mark's vestry book about the location and ages of the Southwest Mountain Chapel and Southwest Mountain Church were ignored or interpreted to fit the traditional location of a chapel in the northwest corner of the county. This location of the oldest house of worship in St. Thomas' Parish, first proposed by Joseph Earnest, was accepted by later historians. Nineteenth-century historians placed it near Cave's Ford or the Indian Mound or Benjamin Cave, Sr.'s eighteenth-century home or Robert Brooking's nineteenth-century home, and twentieth-century historians suggested that remains of this centuries-old house of worship might be a "farm storage barn" or "granary" still standing near the Indian Mound. (Were the nineteenth-century historians aware of this "farm storage building"?) Earnest, Slaughter, Thomas and W. W. Scott said this earliest house of worship in northwest Orange County was replaced by a church, which they called the "old Orange Church," which was later moved to near Ruckersville. Their insistence on calling the New [Orange] Church the second church built in St. Thomas' Parish, may have been because it was closer to their "first church" in northwest Orange County, which they said it replaced, than the Middle or Pine Stake Churches, and because of the antiquity attached to the "old Orange Church" in the nineteenth century. Neither Ulysses P. Joyner, Jr. nor Ann Miller suggested the church which replaced the Southwest Mountain Chapel had any connection with the New (Orange) Church: Joyner did not even mention the Southwest Mountain Church, and Miller said the Southwest Mountain Church was built near the Southwest Mountain Chapel in northwest Orange County.

Although local tradition correctly preserved the memory of a colonial church standing in the northwest corner of Orange County, the evidence presented here proves this church was not the Southwest Mountain Chapel, the second oldest house of worship in the parish, but was the Upper Church, the fourth church built in the parish and the first ordered built by the St. Thomas' vestry. W. W. Scott came close identifying the Upper Church when he said the church "in the Brooking neighborhood" was built shortly after the formation of St. Thomas' Parish; but he identified this church as the Southwest Mountain Chapel. It was J. William Browning, the first and only historian to use court records to identify a church, who correctly named and identified the church built in northwest "Orange" County as the Upper Church, the first church built by the St. Thomas' vesty. This identification and Browning's creative use of court records, published over seven decades ago, was ignored by later historians.

APPENDIX I: SELECTED ORANGE COUNTY, VIRGINIA, COURT ORDERS, 1729–1800

The following road orders appear exactly as published in *Spotsylvania County Road Orders, Orange County Road Orders 1734–1749* and *Orange County Road Orders 1750–1800*. Some orders, which describe churches outside St. Thomas' Parish, are not quoted in full.

3 September 1729 *(SCRO, 39)* **(Southwest Mountain Chapel)**
On Petition of Benjamin Cave for & in behalf of himself and others for a road from the Walnut Branch on y^e. North Side of Rappadan Down the Ridge & to Cross y^e. Rappadan so Down to the South West Mountain Chappell, is granted, And Ordered that the said Benjamin Cave be Overseer thereof, And that all the Tithables which are Situated adjacent on y^e. River Do help him ye s^d. Cave Clear the same –

2 February 1730/31 *(SCRO, 50)* **(Southwest Mountain Chapel)**
On Petition of Benjamin cave to have the road that Comes from black Walnut run a Cross the river to the Mountain Chappel Devided at the river, is granted, and Ordered that Anthony Head be Overseer thereof, And that M^r. Robert Beverlys Tythables and Robert Darings Do Serve under him to help Make And Clear the Said road –

1 June 1731 *(SCRO, 56)* **(Southwest Mountain Chapel)**
On Motion of Robert Beverley Gent. It is Ordered that Anthony Head and his Gang Do Clear the road from the Chappell road over the blue run to his Upper Quarter, and that Benjamin Cave With his gang Do Clear from Poplar bridge to the Rappadan River, and keep the Same in good repair –

1 August 1732 *(SCRO, 67–68)* **(Southwest Mountain Chapel)**
Ordered that the road from the Chappell road to the Upper side of the Blew run Whereof Anthony Head is Overseer be Devided in two precincts and that the Said Head be Continued Overseer of the Upper Part of ye s^d. road and that from the Top of the hill above the blew run to Rippons Quarter, and that all the Tithables above the blew run to Rippons Quarter, and Robt. Dearing and the Tithables at Rippons Quarter Do help him Clear the Same and Ordered that Richard Winslow be appointed Overseer from the hill on the upper Side of the blew run Just below Beverleys Mill to the Chappell road, And that all the Tithables hereafter Mentioned Viz^t. John Rucker & his Tithables,

W^m. Crafords, John Andersons, Henry Downes, Thomas Jacksons, and Richard Winslows. Do help him Clear the Said road –

6 September 1732^A (*SCRO*, 69) **(Great Fork Church)**
On Petition of Philemon Cavenaugh in behalf of himself & others Setting forth the ill Conveniency of their Way already Cleared to ye Parish Church in the fork of Rappahanock and Petitioning for a More Conveniant Way to be Cleared from the fork road above Joseph Colemans into ye s^d. Place appointed for ye s^d. Parish Church. Ordered that Thomas Stanton & George Wheatley Do veiw the Ways & Make report Which is Most Convenients to the Next Court –

6 September 1732^B (*SCRO*, 69–70) **(Southwest Mountain Chapel)**
On Petition of Thomas Jackson & John Rucker in behalf of themselves and Others, to be Discharged from Working under M^r. Richard Winslow Overseer of the Road from the Chapell to the Top of the Hill above Blew Water Run -- Which Road Was granted by the Petition of Robert Beverley Esq. Last Court, and Shewing their being another road & c^a: the Said Petition is refferred to the Consideration of Next Court, and that Robert Beverley Esqr. have Notice given of their being Such a Petition Depending –

7 November 1732 (*SCRO*, 72) **(Southwest Mountain Chapel)**
On the Petition of thomas Jackson and John Rucker for themselves and others, to be released and Discharged from the road Whereof M^r. Richard Winslow is Overseer from the Chappell to the Top of the Hill above blew Water Runk Setting forth that they serve on the road from ffox Point to Crawfords Stone Which is Ten or Eleven Miles Distance the same is granted, and Ordered that they be Discharged from Serveing under the said Winslow On the said road from the Chappell to the Top of Hill above blew Water run –

8 November 1732 (*SCRO*, 72–73) **(Great Fork Church)**
On the Petition of Philemon Cavenaugh in behalf of himself & others Setting forth the ill conveniency of their way allready cleared to the Parrish Church in the fork of Rapahanock & petitioning for a more convenient way to be cleared from the fork road above Joseph Colemans into ye Said place appointed for the Said Parrish Church the last order not being fully complyed with the Same is continued for the Said Thomas Stanton & George Wheatley the Gent^n. appointed P the Court to veiw the ways and make a speciall & fuller report of the nearest & convenients way to the next court –

6 February 1732/33 (*SCRO*, 75) (**Southwest Mountain Chapel**)
On Motion of Robert Beverley Gent It is Ordered that the Tithables under M^r: Winslow Henry Downes George Anderson, William Crawford, William Crosswhite & John Rucker Do Clear the road from the Chappell run over the blew run to the said Beverleys Mill under the s^d: Winslow overseer of the said road –

7 February 1732/33^A (*SCRO*, 75) (**Great Fork Church**)
On Motion of Goodrich Lightfoot Gent for a road to be Cleared from Stantons main road to the place where the Church is to be placed in the fork is granted and George Wheatley is appointed Overseer thereof –

7 February 1732/33^B (*SCRO*, 75) (**Great Fork Church**)
On the petition of Philemon Cavenaugh for himself & others for a road to be Cleared from the fork road a little above Joseph Coleman, to the place appointed for the Church to be built, the Court haveing Considered the Veiwers report, are of oppinion & accordingly order that the petition be dismist –

4 June 1734 (*SCRO*, 88) (**Southwest Mountain Chapel**)
On Motion of Robert Slaughter Gent. for to have a road Cleared from the Glebe in the fork of Rappahannock River, to the South West Mountain Chappel is granted, in order that Christopher Zimmerman be overseer of that part of the S^d. road from S^d. Glebe, to the Island ford, and all the Male tithables that live within four miles of the s^d. Road are ordered to help him Clear & keep in repair the Same, and that Thomas Jones be Overseer of that Part of s^d. road from s^d. Island ford, the old way P W^m. Conico's P Maj^r. John Taliaferros Quarter Called Cattamount, And all the Male tithables y^t. live below y^e. s^d. Quarter (the quarter it Self Excepted) are ordered to Serve Under the S^d. Jones to help him Clear & keep in repair the Same, And that Alexander Waugh be overseer from the s^d. Cattamount Quarter to the South West Mountains Road, and all the Male tithables from the head of the Mountain Run Downwards, are ordered to Serve Under the s^d. Waugh to help him Clear & keep in repair the Same –

1 October 1734 (*SCRO*, 91) (**Great Fork Church and St. Mark's Glebe**)
On Motion of Charles Morgan in behalf of the Ref^d. M^r. John Beckett to have a bridle way from The Gleeb house to y^e. Church & ^{t}. Ordered that Robt. Slaughter Gent. James Kirk & James Pollard or any two of them do View and Lay out the most Convenients way & make report of their proceedings to ye next Court

5 November 1734[A] *(SCRO, 92)* **(Southwest Mountain Chapel)**
Grand Jury Presentments . . . Wee likewise present the overseer of the road from y[e]. South west Mountain Chaple on Fox point Run for not keeping his road in Repair from the s[d]. Chaple to Thomas Chews Mill Run for these two months last past . . .

5 November 1734[B] *(SCRO, 93)* **(Great Fork Church and St. Mark's Glebe)**
James Kirk & James Pollard persons appointed to View & Lay of a bridle way from the Gleebe House in the fork of Rappahannock to the Church (petition for P y[e]. Ref[d]. Joh Bickett) made the following return Vis[t]., At a Court held for Spotsylvania on Tusday October the first 1734, It is ordered on y[e]. petition of Charles Morgin in Behalf of the rev'd M[r]. John Becket to have a bridle way from y[e]. Gleeb house to y[e]. Church the most Convenient we y[e]. Subscribers whose Names are heare Under writen have Begun at y[e]. Gleeb and Marked out a road to y[e]. Church According to y[e]. Worship full Order y[e]. Cort, James Kirk, James Pollard, which said View & return is received P the Court & ordered to be recorded

18 February 1734/35[A] *(OCRO, 5)* **(Southwest Mountain Chapel)**
John Henderson on Pamunkey is hereby appointed Constable from the Southside of the Mountain Road up to the Chappell & it is ordered that the Sheriff Summons the said Henderson to the next Court to be held for this County to be Sworn unto the said Office

18 February 1734/35[B] *(OCRO, 5)* **(Southwest Mountain Chapel)**
Ambrose Jones is hereby appointed Constable on the Northside of the Mountain Road from the Wildernes[s] Bridge up to the Chappell &. it is ordered that the Sheriff Summon the said Jones to the next Court to be held for this County to be Sworn unto the said Office

18 February 1734/35[C] *(OCRO, 7)* **(Southwest Mountain Chapel)**
John Howard is hereby appointed Surveyor of the highways from the Chapple Road to the Rapidan Caves ford and it is ordered that the said John Howard cause the highways to be cleared and the Bridges repaired in the said Precinct according to Law

This road continues to:

18 February 1734/35 *(OCRO, 7)*
James Barber is hereby appointed Surveyor of the highways from the Rapidan River to Charles Blunts Lower path and it is ordered that the

said James Barber cause the highways to be cleared and the Bridges repaired in the said Precinct according to Law

18 February 1734/35 (*OCRO*, 7)
Robert Cave is hereby appointed Surveyor of the highways from Charles Blunts lower path to the Fork of Elk Run and it is ordered that the said Robert Cave cause the highways to be cleared and the Bridges repaired in the said Precinct according to Law

18 February 1734/35 (*OCRO*, 7)
John Garth is hereby appointed Surveyor of the highways from the Fork of Elk Run to Stantons River, and it is ordered that the said John Garth cause the highways to be cleared & the Bridges repaired in the said Precinct according to Law

18 February 1734/35[D] (*OCRO*, 7) **(Upper Chapel)**
Thomas Jackson is hereby appointed Surveyor of the highways from the Chappel to the foot of Offells Mountain, and it is ordered that the said Thomas Jackson cause the highways to be cleared and the Bridges repaired in the said Precinct according to Law.

18 February 1734/35[E] (*OCRO*, 8) **(Southwest Mountain Chapel)**
William Smith is hereby appointed Surveyor of the highways from the Tombs Stone to the Chappell Bridge and it is ordered that the said Smith cause the highways to be cleared & Bridges repaired in the said Precinct according to Law, & it is further ordered that all the male labouring tithables which formerly were under Henry Downs to assist and observe the said Surveyors orders & directions in doing the Same.

18 February 1734/35[F] (*OCRO*, 9) **(Southwest Mountain Chapel)**
James Coward is hereby appointed Surveyor of the highways from the lower side of the Chappel to Chews mill Run & it is ordered that the said James Coward cause the highways to be cleared & the Bridges repaired in the said Precinct according to Law

18 March 1734/35[A] (*OCRO*, 9) **(Churches)**
Ordered that Publick notice be given that the Ferry at Germanna with the plantation be let at the next Court under Such restrictions as are mentioned in the Return that the Gent: that were desired to wait on the Hon:[ble] Col°: Spotswood have returnd into Court & their Return is ordered to be recorded. And it is further ordered that advertisements be set up at the Churches.

18 March 1734/35^B (*OCRO*, 10) **(Southwest Mountain Chapel)**
John Lightfoot Gent is hereby appointed Surveyor of the Highways from the Tomb Stone to the Chappel Bridge in the Room of Wm Smith & it is ordered that the said John Lightfoot cause the highways to be cleared and the Bridges repaired in the said Precinct according to law. And it is further ordered that all the male labouring Tithables belonging to Henry Thornton, William Smith, Thomas Hill, Mr Beale under Jeremiah Bryant James Taylor's Richard Thomas's under George Easham Elisha Daniel & Samuel Drake do assist and Observe the said Surveyors orders and Directions in doing the Same.

16 September 1735^A (*OCRO*, 12) **(Great Fork Church and St. Mark's Glebe)**
Ordered that Christopher Zimmerman and John Kirke with the labouring tithables in their Precincts clear the road that is already marked out from the Glebe to the Church in the Great Fork.

16 September 1735^B (*OCRO*, 12) **(Southwest Mountain Church)**
Its ordered that Alexander Waugh with the tithables in his precinct clear the Road from the Island ford into the Mountain Road that leads to the Mountain Church

18 November 1735^A (*OCRO*, 13) **(Southwest Mountain Church)**
On the Petition of John Barnett for a Road to Church by Richard Thomas' Quarter it is granted him provided he clear Same with his own hands.

18 November 1735^B (*OCRO*, 13) **(Churches)**
Ordered that the Sheriff give publick notice at every Church in this County that the ferry at Germanna is to be let to the Cheapest undertaker that will enter into bond before the Court for duly keeping the same.

16 December 1735 (*OCRO*, 14) **(North Chapel or German Chapel)**
On the Motion of James Barbour Gent for a road from the South West Mountain ffork Chappell to Capt: Bellfields Plantation Its Ordered that He may Clear the Same with his own Tithables and Such as are willing to Assist

17 February 1735/36 (*OCRO*, 15) **(North Chapel or German Chapel)**
Ordered that a road be cleared from the Chappell in the Little fork to Capt: Bellfields Quarter and that Francis Michael by Surveyor thereof and it is further ordered that the tithables in the little fork do clear from

the Chappell to the River and that the tithables at the thoroughfare do clear the rest.

19 October 1736 (*OCRO*, 18) (**North Chapel** or **German Chapel**)
Ordered that Robt. Cave clear the Road with his gang from the lost Mountain to the Chappel.

This road is continued from:

19 October 1736 (*OCRO*, 18)
Ordered that ffrancis Micall with his former gang clear the Road from the German Road to the Lost Mountain

23 April 1737 (*OCRO*, 22) (**North Chapel** or **German Chapel**)
On petitions of M^r: Beckett to have a road from the Gleebe to ye Chappel in the Great fork it is ordered that Francis Slaughter William Strother & John Roberts or any two of them view and lay off the said road and make report thereof to the next Court

22 May 1737 (*OCRO*, 25) (**North Chapel** or **German Chapel**)
The Order for a road from the Gleebe to ye Chappel continued for ye Viewers to make their return.

27 April 1738 (*OCRO*, 31) (**Southwest Mountain Church**)
Zachary Taylor Gent is hereby appointed overseer of ye road from the Church to ye tombstone and its ordered that all ye male tithables of John Rucker John Gaugh George Anderson Wm Crosthwait Robert Adams Hezekiah Rhods Wm Rhods John Davison Samuel Drake Zach^y Taylor James Taylor Danl McCarty Wm Hawkins Wm Smith Wm Bell Robt: Bickers John Collins Jeremiah Dare and Charles Steuart work on ye same & that they be hereby exempted from all other roads And its further ordered that the said Zachary Taylor cause the Highways to be cleared & the bridges repaired in the said precint according to Law.

27 September 1739 (*OCRO*, 40) (**Southwest Mountain Church**)
Ordered that the road petitioned for by the Inhabitants of Pomunkey be made according as laid off by Zachary Taylor George Taylor & John Rucker Gent vizt to begin at pleasant run and to continue up the road near the Course the road runs, crossing Terrys run at John Griffins ford thence along the old path crossing the river at Thomas Cooks ford thence up the ridge to about three miles from the Church thence the nighest way into the mountain road right ag^t Capt: John Ruckers And that M^r: Claytons John Vivins tithables and all the tithables in the fork

of pomunkey/: excluding Charles Steavens's David Caves and Abraham Mayfields:/ do Assist in Clearing the Same & be exempted from the old road And John Brockman is hereby made Overseer of ye s^d road And its further ordered that ye s^d John Brockman cause the s^d road to be cleared & bridges to be made in ye sd road where Occasion shall be And that he keep the said road with the said tithables in repair according to Law.

28 March 1740 (*OCRO*, 45) (Great Fork Church)
Ordered that all Col^o: Spotswoods Tannents below Hungary run that were formerly under Charles Morgan together with Phillip Claytons tithables work on a road from Mountpony to the Church under the said Charles Morgan who is hereby appointed Overseer of ye said road And its ordered that he cause the highways to be cleared & bridges repaired in ye s^d precinct according to Law & that they be exempted from all other roads.

22 May 1740 (*OCRO*, 46) (Southwest Mountain Church)
On the petition of John Ingram Thomas Sims & others for a Bridle way from their Neighbourhood to the Mountain Church Its ordered that Benj^a Porter Richard Kemp and Wm Davison lay of ye nearest best & Most convenient way that can be found to the aforesaid Church & make return of their proceedings to ye next Court.

28 November 1740 (*OCRO*, 52) (Southwest Mountain Church)
On the Petition of John Ingram & Thos Sims for a bridle way from the Nighbourhood to ye Church Its ordered that the s^d Ingram have Liberty with the help of those that are willing to clear the Same.

28 May 1741 (*OCRO*, 56) (Southwest Mountain Church)
George Taylor Gent by his petition Setting forth that he & many of his Neighbours are in great want of a road convenient to Church that they have mark'd every good way but dare not clear it without an order of Court Its ordered that Zachary Taylor & Richard Thomas Gent view the road petitioned for & make return of their proceedings to ye next Court.

26 June 1741 (*OCRO*, 57) (Southwest Mountain Church)
The order for Viewing the road petitioned for by George Taylor Gent being returned into Court by Zachary Taylor and Richard Thomas Gent with a report thereon that they had viewed the Most convenient way from the Inhabitants near the Mouth of ye Robinson to the Church at the Mountains Its ordered to be cleared according to the return and Joseph Thomas who hereby is appointed Overseer of the Same is

ordered to clear the Same with his and George Taylors tithables who are exempted from all other roads.

27 August 1741 (*OCRO*, 59) **(Chapel in Frederick County)**
George Hobson having put in a pet[n] in behalf of ye Inhabitants of the North side of Opecken for a road from the most convenientest fford over Sherundo at Ashbys Bent & from thence the Best way to and between the Lands of John Littler and John ffrost to the Chappell house & from thence to Evan Watkins ferry upon potomack Its ordered that Morgan Bryan Arthur Buchannan & John ffrost or any two of them View y[e] s[d] road pet[d] for & make report of their proceedings to y[e] next Court.

28 November 1741 (*OCRO*, 63) **(St. Mark's Glebe)**
Ordered on the Motion of Captn Robert Green that the people on y[e] Mountain Run clear ye road from M[r]: Easthams to the Gleebe And that the Tithables of ffrancis Slaughter Gent of Wm Strother Christopher Zimmerman John Newport Charles Morgan Bryan Thornton James Conner W[m] Lynch Minor Will Jacob Miller Frederick Cobler W[m] Watts Tho[s] Watts James Steward James Chissum W[m] Pannell Daniel Underwood Jeremiah Strother Roger Topp Joseph Botttom W[m] Smith & John Lowing clear M[r]: ffinlassons Road under Tho[s] Wright their Overseer who is hereby orderd to clear y[e] same & keep the bridges of y[e] s[d] road in repair according to Law with the afd tithables.

26 February 1741/42 (*OCRO*, 65) **(Chapel in Frederick County)**
On the order for viewing and laying off a road petitioned for by Hobson & Others Morgan Bryan John ffrost and Arthur Buchannan the persons orderd to lay of y[e] s[d] road made their return as followeth In pursuance of an order of Court We have viewed and laid off a road from Evan Watkins fferry by a Course of Marked trees to the head of y[e] ffaling Spring thence to Roger Turners thence to Edward Beasons over the Taskerora Branch thence to Joseph Evans Spring head thence to the Middle Creek thence to New Chappell Thence by the head of Evan Thomas Spring head thence to a Corner White oak between the lands of John Littler and John ffrost thence along the said Line to y[e] Corner South Eastward thence to Secorns Licks thence to Opecken Creek & Crossing the Same just above John Neils Mill Branch thence to the Spout run by Edges Cabbin thence to the King's road that leads from Just Hites to Shennindo & to fall into the Same by John Kerseys plantation near Shennendoford We also recommend . . . [*continues with tithables ordered to work on this road*]

25 March 1742^A (*OCRO*, 67) **(Upper Church or Southwest Mountain Church)**
Ordered that the people under John Duglass clear the Lower part of ye road to ye Church and that Anthony Head clear ye upper part of ye s^d road with the tithables under them & its further ordered that the cause ye s^d road to be cleared & the bridges repaired in the said precincts according to Law.

25 March 1742^B (*OCRO*, 67) **(Southwest Mountain Church)**
Ordered that the road from David Caves Church path to George Smiths Path be turned & that John Thomas & Daniel White view and lay of ye same the Most convenientest Way for rolling according to ye pet^n of Charles Curtis Gent & that Justiphonica Smith clear ye Same with his gang when Laid off & make report to the next Court.

26 March 1742 (*OCRO*, 68) **(St. Mark's Glebe)**
Ordered that the tithables of Saml Ball Gent at Mountpony Wm Strothers M^m Buckners John Cattletts David McMurrins Benj^a Taylors Wm Johnsons Col^o Carters John Buttlers Francis Strothers Nicholas Gunnills & John Weatheralls work on the New Road from Mr. Easthams road in the fork to the Gleebe under John Cattlett Gent their Overseer & they are ordered to keep ye s^d road in repair according to Law.
See **23 January 1745/46.**

27 May 1742^A (*OCRO*, 68–69) **(Upper Church)**
On the Petition of Alex^r Cleaveland Its ordered that John Askew Lawrance ffranklin & John ffoster or any two of them view and Lay of the convenientest way for a road from the New Church into Anthony Heads road & make return of their proceedings to the next Court.

27 May 1742^B (*OCRO*, 69) **(Southwest Mountain Church)**
Ordered that the Gang under Edward Tinsley Overseer of the Courthouse road from Porters to Crosthwaits clear that part of the road to Church that Taylors & Thomas's people were ordered to clear.

28 May 1742 (*OCRO*, 70) **(Chapel in Frederick County)**
More about the **27 August 1741** *and* **26 February 1741/42** *road.*

22 July 1742 (*OCRO*, 72) **(Church near Bloodworth's Road)**
On the petition of William Russell Gent for a road from the German road where the Courthouse road divides itself to the next [*"new" on* **24 September 1742** *order*] road called Bloodworths road near the Church

its ordered that Christopher Zimmerman and Richard Wright view lay of and mark the said road & make report to the next court of their proceedings.

24 July 1742 (*OCRO*, 73) **(Chapel in Frederick County)**
More about the **27 August 1741** *and* **26 February 1741/42** *road.*

24 September 1742 (*OCRO*, 75) **(Church near Bloodworth's Road)**
More about the **22 July 1742** *road.*.

29 January 1742/43^A (*OCRO*, 80) **(Upper Chapel)**
Thos Jackson Junr is hereby appointed overseer of ye road from the old Chappell to Jacksons Mill in ye room of Richard Mauldin and its ordered that he Cause the said road to be cleared & the bridges to be repaired in ye s^d precinct according to Law.

29 January 1742/43^B (*OCRO*, 80) **(Church near Bloodworth's Road)**
More about the **22 July 1742** *and* **24 September 1742** *road.*

26 February 1742/43 (*OCRO*, 81–82) **(Upper Church)**
The order for ye road petitioned for by Cleaveland be returned its ordered that the new order issue according to the direction of ye pet^rs vizt that Jno Askew Lawrance ffranklin & Jno ffoster or any two of them view and lay off a road out of the James River Mountain road near or about Head Lynch's house to go by the Arbour the nearest & Best way that is to be found into Anthony Heads road about half a mile below ye Church and that the make return of their proceedings to ye next Court.

26 May 1743^A (*OCRO*, 84) **(Southwest Mountain Church)**
Thos Scott Senr is hereby appointed overseer of the road from the Southwest mountain Church to James Cowards, in the room of James Coward afd and its ordered that he Cause the said road to be kept in repair according to Law.

26 May 1743^B (*OCRO*, 84) **(Great Fork Church)**
A Grandjury for the body of this County . . . do present That the road from the Mountain run bridge to the Church is out of repair and that we do present Wm Russell the overseer for ye same . . .
See 24 July 1740 p. 48.

27 May 1743^A (*OCRO*, 85) **(Church near Bloodworth's Road)**
The **22 July 1742** *petition is approved.*

27 May 1743[B] (*OCRO*, 86) **(Upper Church)**
John Askew Lawrance ffranklin & John ffoster having on the order for
viewing and laying off the road petitioned for by Alex[r] Cleaveland &
others to go out of the James River Mountain road near or about Head
Lynches house by y[e] harbour the nearest way Into Anthony Heads road
about half a mile below the Church made their return that they had laid
of and Marked the said road Its ordered that the said road be cleared
according to y[e] Viewers return and Its further ordered that ffrancis
Wisdom John Douglass Alex[r] Cleaveland Jun[r]: John Cleaveland
Thomas Ballard Henry Hanes Benj[a] ffranklin Edward Coffee Alex[r]
Cleaveland Sen[r]: John Snell John ffoster John Haskew And all the male
labouring tithables in y[e] s[d] precinct help to Clear y[e] same under
Lawrance ffrenklin who is hereby their Overseer & its also ordered that
he with said tithables cause ye same to be cleared according to Law.

25 August 1743 (*OCRO*, 89) **(German Chapel)**
On the Petition of John Zimmerman & other German Inhabitants for a
bridle Road to their Chappell Ordered that they clear such bridle Road
at their PP expence not prejudicial to any Plantation.

24 November 1743 (*OCRO*, 91) **(German Chapel)**
On y[e] Petition of Mich[l] Claure and others for the former Path to the
German Chappel to be kept open by the Petitioners the same is granted.

25 November 1743 (*OCRO*, 92) **(Upper Church)**
On y[e] Petition of Henry Downes Gent & others that the Road from
Blue run Road to y[e] upper Church is impassible, Its Ordered that the
same be Repayred by W[m]. Lucass and John Asquese's Gang and Henry
Downes Gent is hereby appointed Overseer of the s[d] Road who is
ordered wth said gangs to keep the same in repayr According to Law.

26 January 1743/44 (*OCRO*, 93) **(Southwest Mountain Church)**
On the Petition of John Lucas for the Road from the Church to the
Tombstone to be kept in repayr by the several persons hereafter named
Viz[t] Tully Choice W[m] McDonagh William Rhodes Hezekia Rhoades
Timothy Crosthwait John Goss W[m]. Goldin, M[rs] Rucker. W[m]. Bell M[rs].
Hills Quarter M[r] Zachary Taylor M[r] Erasmus Taylor Sam[l] Drake M[r].
Jo[s] Morton M[r]. James Taylors Quarter Thom[s] Smith Major Fran[s]
Talliaferro's Qu[r] where Hawkins lived John Fennele M[r]. John
Talliaferroe's Quarter Rob[t] Bickers John Walker John Collins Jeremiah
Dear & Bechnall Alvasson Its therefore ordered by the Court that the
sev[l] persons abovenamed do Clear and keep the s[d] Road in repair under
the direction of the s[d] John Lucas Overseer thereof.

26 April 1744 (*OCRO*, 97) **(Little Fork Chapel)**
On the Petition of Thomas Washburn & others for a Road from above
the Chappel in the Little fork to Hedgmans Mill & for the Tithables
below Indian Run to work thereon Its Ordered that Robert Green Gent
Robt Eastham Gent, Wm Tapp & John Bridges or any two of them do
view and Lay off the same & that the former Overseer imediately after
Layd off Clear & repayr the same with the Tithables Petitioned for to
work thereon & the former Tithables under s^d. Overseer.

29 June 1744 (*OCRO*, 101) **(Great Fork Church)**
Ordered That Peter Russell Overseer Do with his Gang Clear from the
Main Road to the Fork Church & from the Church upward to the Main
Road.

26 July 1744 (*OCRO*, 101) **(Probably Little Fork Chapel)**
Ordered That that Part of the Road that goes from Nathaniel Hedgmans
Plantation To Easthams Chapple as is commonly called be kept open
And that M^r. Charles Dewit be Overseer of the same and that he Clear
it wth the former Gang that belong to the former Road.

22 November 1744 (*OCRO*, 104) **(Middle Church)**
A Grandjury for the Body of this County . . . Brought in their
Presentments as Followeth: . . . Wee present the Overseer of the road
from the Middle Church to Crawfords Tomb Stone for not Keeping the
said Road in repair.

23 November 1744 (*OCRO*, 105) **(Upper Church)**
On the motion of Henry Down Gent for Being Discharged from
Overseeing the road from the Blue Run to the upper Church and its
ordered that Phillip Bush oversee the same and that the former
Tythables Do work under the said Bush.

24 January 1744/45 (*OCRO*, 106) **(Upper Church)**
On Petition of John Foster in Behalf of himself & Others for a road to
be Layd of from the new Church road into Blew run road a little Below
the three Springs its ordered that Jno. Askew Alex^a. Cleaveland and
John Snell or any two or more of them Do view and Lay of a road the
most best and Convenienest way and make return to the next Court of
their Proceedings.

23 May 1745 (*OCRO*, 107) **(Upper Church)**
The Grand Jury Returned into Court and made the following
Presentments . . . We also present the Overseer of the highway from the

upper Church to Henry Downs's for not keeping the said way in repair.

27 June 1745 (*OCRO*, 110) **(Upper Church)**
Ordered that Benjamin Cave James Barber and Henry Downs or any two of them do Sometime between this and the Next Court go to and View the way from the New Church Road into blue Run Road a little above the three Springs and a Way to be Shewn to them by William Lucas and Report to the Court which is the most Convenient way for a Publick Road.

22 August 1745 (*OCRO*, 112) **(Upper Church)**
Alexander Cleaveland John Haskey and John Snell having Viewed the way from the New Church Road into the blue run Road a little above the three Springs according to the Order made in January Court last made their report in these Words, In Obedience to the within Order We the Subscribers have Mett Viewed and laid off and Markt out the Road mentioned in the within order according as within to us is Commanded Alexander Cleaveland John Haskey John Snell whereupon it is Ordered that the said Ways be from henceforth be established and that John ffoster be hereby appointed Surveyor of the said Road and it is Ordered that he Cause the said Road to be cleared that John Haskey John Snell William Lucas Junr. John ffoster Benjamin Franklin John ffoster Junr. Lawrance Franklin William Lucas Senr. and Alexander Cleveland and their Respective Male Tythables Do attend and obey the said Overseer in Clearing the Same and when the said Road is Cleared to keep the same in repair and it is further ordered that the s^d Overseer set up posts of Direction if Necessary according to Law.

27 September 1745 (*OCRO*, 113) **(Upper Church)**
The Presentment of the Grand Jury against Philip Bush overseer of the Road from the upper Church to Henry Downes's is Dismissed.

28 November 1745 (*OCRO*, 115) **(Great Fork Church)**
The Grand Jury returning into Court the following Presentments . . . We also present the Overseers of the Road from the upper End of Mountpony Down to the fork Church for not keeping their Road in Repair.

23 January 1745/46 (*OCRO*, 116) **(St. Mark's Glebe)**
James Conner is by the Court appointed Overseer of the Road from the Glebe in Saint Marks Parrish to Roberts's Ordinary in the Room of John Catlett Gent Deced and It is Ordered that he set up posts of Direction if Necessary and keep the said Road in repair.

27 March 1746 (*OCRO*, 116) **(Little Fork Chapel)**
James Spilman by the Court appointed Overseer of the Road in the Little Fork from Hedgmans Ford on the North River up to the said Little Fork Chappell in the Room of Charles Dewitt who is Discharged from that Office and the Gang Ordered to be under him are [*tithables to work on road*]

22 May 1746 (*OCRO*, 119) **(Southwest Mountain Church)**
Thomas Newman is by the Court appointed Overseer of the Road from the south west Mountain Church to the Tomstone in the Room of John Lucas and it is Ordered that the Gangs which were under the said Lucas attend the said Newman and obey his Directions in clearing & keeping the said Road in repair and that he cause Posts of Directions to be set up where Necessary.

26 July 1746 (*OCRO*, 122) **(Great Fork Church)**
The Presentment of the Grand jury against the Overseer of the upper end of Road from Mountpony to the Fork Church is Dismissed.

26 September 1746 (*OCRO*, 123) **(Pine Stake Church)**
Ordered that Stephen J K Smith George Smith Richard Bradley and Joseph Reynolds or any two of them do some time between this and the Next Court go to and View the way from the Pine stake Church into the Road that Leads to Stark's Bridge and report to the Court accordingly.

26 February 1746/47 (*OCRO*, 126) **(German [Chapel] Church)**
Ordered That a Road be cleared from Fleshmans bridge the way formerly Cleared to the bridge below The old German Mill near the german Church and that John Zimmerman be Surveyor thereof & The hands formerly on the same are to attend and obey the said Surveyor in clearing and keeping The same in repair and that the said Surveyor cause Posts of Direction to be set up Where necessary.

28 May 1747^A (*OCRO*, 129) **(Middle Church)**
Ordered that the road from the middle Church in S^t: Thomas's Parish to the Place Called the Tomb Stone be Divided with respect to the Surveyor thereof & that Thomas Newman who is the Present Surveyor of the same Continue Surveyor from the Church to Poplar Spring and that his People and all above them Work under him on that Part of the road & That the rest of the gang that Worked on the said Road work on the lower Part over which John Finny is hereby Appointed Surveyor And It is ordered that the said Surveyors cause the said way to be keept in repair acording to Law.

28 May 1747^B *(OCRO*, 130) **(Tenent's Church)**
Ordered that Frances Michael Robert Levil Jonathan Pratt & Spencer Bobo or any two or moor of them do some time between this & the next Court go to & vew the way from the old German road by John Wilhites to the Church at Tennants Old field & report to the Court the most Convenient way for a road.

27 August 1747 *(OCRO*, 132) **(Tenent's Church)**
The **28 May 1747^B** *road is ordered cleared.*

23 June 1748 *(OCRO*, 137) **(Upper Church)**
Ordered That James Barbour Gent Joseph Rogers & Thomas Rucker or any two of them do some time between this & the next Court go to & view the Way from the River to the upper Church in Saint Thomas's Parish through the Lands of Darby Quin & report to the Court the most convenient way for a Bridle Way.

23 March 1748/49 *(OCRO*, 140) **(Tenent's Church)**
Ordered that Henry Field Gent John Kines & John Zimmerman or any two of them do some time between this and the next Court go to & view the Way from Robert King's Plantation to Tenant's Church & report to the next Court the most convenient Way for a Road.

22 June 1749 *(OCRO*, 140) **(Middle Church)**
Ordered that Benjamin Cave Gent do take a List of the Tithables in this County on the South Side of the Road he lives on up to the Pamunky Road by the middle Church.

22 March 1749/50 *(OCRO*, 144) **(Upper Church)**
Richard Sebree is appointed overseer of the Road from the upper Church to Heads Ford & that he with the hands under John Snell keep the same in Repair & that they be exempted from working on any other Road.

24 March 1749/50 *(OCRO*, 145) **(Upper Church or Middle Church)**
On the Petition of Henry Downs &° Ordered that Joseph Thomas Zach. [torn page] & Eras. Tayl[or] do view the most Conven^t. way for a Road to go from below Crosthwaits by [torn] to the Road that goes by the Church & to make report to the next Court whether the same [same torn page].

24 May 1750 *(OCRO*, 5) **(Middle Church)**
Ordered that John Embry be Overseer of the Road from the Church to

the Road by Starks bridge and that he with Isaac Bradbourns, Joseph Woolfolks John Grays, Joseph Graves John Henderson Edward Carters John Stevens, Thomas Merry and Reubin Daniel Male Labouring tithables clear the same & keep it in Repair –

26 July 1750 (*OCRO*, 7) **(Upper Church)**
On the Petition of the Reverend Mr Marshall for a Road to be cleared from the Glebe by M^r. Tinsleys over the mouth of Baylors Run into the Main Road that leads by Capt. Downs Mill as the most convenient way for the Neighbours by him to pass to the uper Church & to the said Mill, it is Ordered that Duncan Bohannon Edward Tinsley and William Pendleton view the same & if they find it Convenient for a Road to be there, then to Mark out the same & make report thereof to the Next Court –

22 November 1750 (*OCRO*, 9) **(Middle Church)**
Grand Jury Presentments The Overseer for not seting up boards of directions at the fork of the pamunkey Road below the Church . . .

24 January 1750/51[A] (*OCRO*, 10) **(Middle Church)**
Charles Curtis Gent is appointed Surveior of the Highway from Spotsylvania County line to the Main Road below the Middle Church in the Room of Richard Bradley & that he with the Gang that was under the said Bradley do clear & keep the said Road in Repair –

24 January 1750/51[B] (*OCRO*, 11) **(Upper Church)**
Ordered that a Bridge be built over the Beverdam Run below the upper Church and that Joseph Thomas Taverner Beale and Henry Downs Gent or any two of them do let out & agree with workmen to build the same –

28 February 1750/51 (*OCRO*, 12) **(Pine Stake Church)**
On the Petition of Benjamin Cave Gent it is Ordered that a Road be cleared from the Main Road by Hardins Quarter to the Pine Stake Church and that the Male Labouring Tithables at the said Hardins Quarter, at Fleets Quarter at Neels Quarter, Edward Haylys, George Bledsoe, James Mitchel, John Hayley, Thomas Gahagon Benjamin Caves Philip Singleton & Daniel Singletons do clear the Same & that Thomas Gahagon be Overseer of the said Road –

23 May 1751[A] (*OCRO*, 13) **(Middle Church)**
Grand Jury Presentments . . . We present the Overseer of the Road from the Midle Church to poplar Spring for not puting Sign posts according to Law

23 May 1751^B (*OCRO*, 13) (Middle Church)
Grand Jury Presentments . . . We present the overseer of the Road from Caves ford to the Middle Chuch for not keeping their Several parts of the said Road in repair by the Information of John Buford . . .

23 May 1751^C (*OCRO*, 14) (Middle Church)
Thomas Chew Gent is appointed to take the List of Tithables in this County below Blue run as low as the Pamunky road below the Middle Church & aCross to the mouth of the Robinson –

27 February 1752 (*OCRO*, 17) (Middle Church)
Ordered that the Bridge over the Church run by Edward Smiths be rebuilt or repaired at the County Charge and that Thomas Chew, Charles Curtis & Joseph Thomas Gent or any Two of them do let out the same at Publick Auction & agree with the undertakers for the Building the same –

28 May 1752 (*OCRO*, 18) (Upper Church)
William Lucas is appointed overseer of the Road from the uper Church down to the Main road above Beverleys Mill in the Room of Henry Downs and that he with the Gang that was under the said Downs keep the said Road in Repair –

22 February 1753 (*OCRO*, 22) (Upper Church)
On the Petition of John Foster for an Order for a Road to be Cleared out of the Road below William Lucas Junr. over the Marsh Run the Most Convenientest way to the upper Church Ordered that John Jones & John Duglass do Veiw the same & make Report to the Court of the Convenience or Ill convenience Attending the Same –

26 April 1753 (*OCRO*, 23) (Unidentifiable)
Robert Slaughter is Appointed Surveyor of the High Way in the Room of Battaile Harrison & that he with the Gang that was under the s^d Battaile except the Widow Gordens & the s^d Battaile Tith^s. Clear & keep the same in Repair and that the said Slaughters, Widow Ruckers, Peter Ruckers and William Goldings Male Tith^s. work in the Clearing of the said Road & be exempted from working on the Road below the Church –

25 May 1753 (*OCRO*, 25) (St. Thomas' Glebe)
Ordered that Duncan Bohanon with the Gang that Clears the road from Barnits ford down to the Main Road to Fredericksburg do also Clear the Way from the Glebe into the said Road by the old School house –

25 April 1754[A] (*OCRO*, 29) **(Middle Church)**
Taverner Beale Gent is appointed to take the list of Tithables in the County from Terrys Run bridge up the Road to the Main Road below the Church & all on the South side the said main Road up to the Blue Run to the plant[n]. where Francis Wisdom lived

25 April 1754[B] (*OCRO*, 29) **(Middle Church)**
James Madison Gent is apointed to take the list of Tith[s] in this County from the Blue Run down to the mouth of the Robinson & aCross to the head of the Mountain Run Between the River & the Road from below the Church up to where Francis Wisdom formerly lived –

23 May 1754 (*OCRO*, 31) **(Middle Church)**
Ordered that the Bridge over the Church Run be added to the Road that Thomas Newman is overseer of & that the said Newman keep the said Bridge in Repair –

28 March 1755 (*OCRO*, 35) **(Middle Church)**
Ordered that Reubin Harris Surveyor of the Lower part of the Road from the Middle Church down the fork of Pamunky With the Gang under him Join with Malica Chiles Surveyor of the uper part of the said Road in each of their Gang Making a bridge over the Run by the said Church –

25 April 1755[A] (*OCRO*, 36) **(Upper Church or Middle Church or Pine Stake Church)**
The Veiwers of the road Petitioned for by Jeremiah Morton Gent that leads from John Christophers to the old Court house to be turned to go Between the Plantation of Crouchers & Williams, having made their report that the Convenientest & best way for the said Road to go Between the said Crouchers & Williams's plantations in to the road that leads to Fred[h]. & the Church and it is therefore Ordered that the road be made to go that way –
The "road that leads to Fred[h]. & the Church", i.e., Route 20, could re-fer to the Middle, the Upper or the Pine Stake Church since all were near Route 20. But the closest church to the "old Court house" (be-tween Somersville and Raccoon Ford from 1737 to1749) was the Pine Stake Church.

25 April 1755[B] (*OCRO*, 36) **(Middle Church)**
Taverner Beale Gent is Appointed to take the list of Tith[s]. in this County from Terrys Run Bridge up the Road to the Church & all on the South side of the Main Road up to the Blue Run to the plantation where

Francis Wisdom forrmerly Lived –

22 May 1755 (*OCRO*, 37) **(Middle Church)**
Grand Jury Presentments ag^t Daniel Singleton & the Overseer of the
road from Starks bridge to the Church . . .

26 June 1755^A (*OCRO*, 38) **(Upper Church)**
On the Petition of the Rev^d. Mungo Marshall for a Road to be cleared
from the Gleebe over Baylors Run into the Road that go's to Beverleys
Mill the Most convenientest way for his going to the Upper Church it is
Ordered that Peter Rucker William Golding Thomas Newman & Phil.
Eastin or any three of them being first Sworn before some Justice for
this County faithfully & impartially to veiw the same do go & veiw the
said Intended Way & Make report to the Court of the Convenience &
inconvenience attending the same –

26 June 1755^B (*OCRO*, 39) **(Middle Church)**
Upon the Presentments of the Grand Jury against Malachi Chiles
Surveyor of the Road from the Middle Church down toward Starks
bridge for not keeping the said Road in repair the said Chiles being
heard it is Considered by the Court that he forfeit & pay to our Soveign
Lord the King fifteen shillings according to Law & that he pay the Cost
of this presentment

27 May 1756 (*OCRO*, 44) **(Probably Middle Church)**
John Mallory is Appointed overseer of the Road from the Ridge above
Wormleys Quarter up to the Church road & that he with the Gang that
works on that part of the road Clear & keep the Same in repair –

22 September 1757 (*OCRO*, 50–51) **(Pine Stake Church)**
Richard Thomas Gent. Stephen Smith & Stephen I. K. Smith who were
appointed & Sworn to veiw the Way from Fredericksburg road by
Hardins old field to join the road from Garnets folly to Spotsylvania
Line having made their report that the same is a Levell way, it is
therefore ordered that the same be Cleared as laid off by the Veiwers to
Spotsylvania to meet the road from the s^d. Line to Garnets folly & the
following Persons are appointed to assist in the opening & Clearing the
said till the same be opened, Viz^t. Daniel Singleton, Philip Singleton
John Bledsoe, Geo Bledsoe, James Mitchell, Joseph Rennolds Samuel
Rice, John Wright, Robert Lancaster the Male Labouring Tith^s. at
Fleets Quarter at John Conners at Braxtons Quarter at Thos. Haleys &
also the Gang that works on the Road from the Poplar Spring down to
the Tomb Stone & with those that work on the roads above Capt. Caves

to the pine Stake Church & that Philip Singleton be overseer of the same –

25 November 1757 (*OCRO*, 53) **(Middle Church)**
On the motion of Zachary Lewis Gent for the way the Road goes up the Hill on the South side of the Run below the Middle Church to be turned so as to shun the said hill ordered that Zachᵃ. Taylor James Wagoner, John Lea & Thoˢ. Burgess or any three of them being first sworn as the Law directs do veiw the said Way and make report to the Court of the Conveniences & Inconveniences attending the Same –

23 February 1758 (*OCRO*, 54) **(Middle Church)**
The Persons appointed to Veiw the way for the Road to be turned on the South Side the Bridge below the Middle Church to shun the hill where the Road now goes, they have reported that the Most convenient way for the said Road to go is on the uper side a small Velly & it is Ordered that the Overseer of the said Road with the gang under him clear the same as Reported by the said Veiwers & keep the same in repair –

25 May 1758 (*OCRO*, 56) **(Middle Church)**
On the Motion of Richard Woolfold overseer of the Road that goes from the Church a Cross the River down to Pamunkey that his gang is not able to make a bridge over the sᵈ. River & prays the same be built at the County Charge, Thomas Chew Rowland Thomas & Richᵈ. Thomas Gent undertakes to Veiw the place where the sᵈ. Bridge is to be erected & if they think the same is Necessary to be built at County Charge that they let out the same to be built & take bond & security for the same –

26 October 1758 (*OCRO*, 58) **(Upper Church)**
Ordered that Thomas Chew & James Madison Gent let out at Public Auction the building a New or repairing the old bridge over the Beverdam run below the upper Church –

24 May 1759 (*OCRO*, 61) **(Probably Pine Stake Church)**
Ordered that all the Male Labouring Tithables at Capt. Caves & John Wrights work on the Church Road & that the said Wright be Overseer of the same & with the sᵈ. Gang clear & keep the said in Repair –

22 November 1759 (*OCRO*, 64) **(Middle Church)**
Zachary Taylor Peter Rucker Thoˢ. Burgess & John Lea or any three of them are appointed to Veiw the best way for the road on the South side Run below the Church to be turned up the hill they being first Sworn as

the Law directs & to make report thereof to the Court –

27 March 1760 (*OCRO*, 67) **(Middle Church)**
Ordered that Johnny Scott with the Gang his is overseer of clear the road down as Low as the Bridge at the Main Run by the Middle Church

26 June 1760 (*OCRO*, 69) **(Middle Church)**
Thomas Burrus is appointed overseer of the road from the Church bridge down the fork of the s^d. Road in the room of Richard Woolfolk & that he with the Gang that was under the said Woolfolk clear & keep the s^d. road in repair –

25 September 1760 (*OCRO*, 70) **(Pine Stake Church)**
On the Motion of Richard Thomas Gent for Leave for a way to be cleared from John Pendletons to the Pine Stake Church, it is Ordered that Elijah Morton Gent, Stephen Smith, Stephen I. K. Smith, & Jos. Chandler or any three of them being Sworn as the Law directs do Veiw the Most Convenient Way for the s^d. Road to be cleared & make report to the Court of the Conveniences & inconveniences attending the same

23 April 1761 (*OCRO*, 73) **(Middle Church)**
Zachary Taylor is appointed Overseer of the Road in the Room of John Lea & that he with the Gang that was under the s^d. Lea & his own Male Labouring tith^s. Added thereto Clear the s^d. Road from the Lower part of his precinct up to the foot of the hill above the Church including the Bridges & Causeway & keep in Repair –

28 May 1761 (*OCRO*, 74) **(New [Orange] Church)**
On the Petition of William Bell Gent for a Bridle Way to be Cleared from his house to the Chapple Ordered that John Goodall, James Beasley Matthew Creed & John Roberts or any three of them being first sworn as Law directs do Veiw the way Petitioned for & Make their report to the court of the Convenience & inconvenience attending the Same –

24 July 1761 (*OCRO*, 75) **(New [Orange] Church)**
The Persons appointed to Veiw the way Pet^d. for by Capt. Bell for a Bridle Way from his house to the Chappel, having reported the same a good & Convenient way & not prejudicial to any body it is Ordered that he have Leave to clear the Same as Mark'd by the s^d. Veiwers –

27 November 1761 (*OCRO*, 75) **(Middle Church)**
Ordered that Rowland Thomas Richard Thomas & James Walker Gent

or any two of them Veiw the place where the Road that leads to Pamunkey Crosses the run below the Middle Church & if they think it Necessary that a bridge ought to be Built over the Run there at the County Charge to let the same out at Public Aution –

28 October 1762 (*OCRO*, 78) **(New [Orange] Church)**
The Way Petitioned for by William Bell for a Way to be cleared from his house to the Chappel not being yet cleared it is Ordered that W^m. Cox & James Beasley with the Gangs they are overseers of do Once clear the said Way –

25 November 1762 (*OCRO*, 78) **(Middle Church)**
On the Petition of George Roebuck John Noel &c for a Road to be cleared along John Noels church path from the Pamunkey road below the Middle Church, heading Embres Mill run & crossing the white Oak below Richard Martins, to the New Ridge Tract & down the Ridge to Saml. Thompsons ford upon the Northana, Ordered that Peter Rucker, William Webb, Joseph Rogers & John Lea, or any three of them being first Sworn as the Law Directs do Veiw the Most Convenientest way for the s^d. Road to go & that they make to the Court of the Conveniences & inconveniences Attending the Same –

27 January 1763 (*OCRO*, 79) **(St. Thomas' Glebe)**
On the Petition of Benjamin Porter for a Road to be cleared from the Gleebe plantation to his Mill the Most Convenientest way for Carts to go to the said Mill it is Ordered that Rowland Thomas Gent. Edward Tinsley Geo. Smith & John Grigsby or any three of them being first Sworn as the Law directs do Veiw the most Convenientest way for the said Road to go & make report to the Court of the Conveniences & inconveniences attend^g. the Same –

24 March 1763^A (*OCRO*, 80) **(St. Thomas' Glebe)**
The Veiwers of the way Petitioned for by Ben. Porter for a Road to his Mill have reported the Most Convenient Way is to continue the old Path from the Glebe Road which leads by Zachary Gibs Lease into Smiths Mill road & so to the Mill which is not Prejudicial to any body therefore it is Ordered that the said Road be cleared as above mentioned –

24 March 1763^B (*OCRO*, 81) **(New [Orange] Church)**
Ordered that John White William Scott James Griffin & Rich^d. Griffin or any three of them being first Sworn as the Law directs do Veiw the Most Convenient & best Way for a Road to be cleared from the

Chapple to Join the Road Cleared by Culpeper County Near Conways Quarter & make report to the Court of the Conveniences or inconveniences of the Same –

28 April 1763[A] (*OCRO*, 82) (New [Orange] Church)
The Persons appointed to Veiw the road to be cleared from the Chapple to Joyn the Road cleared by Culpeper County near Conways Quarter, having made their report & laid off & Marked the best Way for the s[d]. Road to be made, it is Ordered that a road be cleared as marked by the Veiwers & that the Male labouring Tithables at M[r]. Stanards Quarter M[r]. Thorntons & M[rs]. Conways Quarter, Tho[s]. Walkers, Thomas Walkers ju[n]. William Sims, Charles Walkers, James Powell, John Powell, W[m]. Massey, John Canterburry, John Mayfield, Stephen Shifflet James Walker, James Shepherd, John White Joshua Jackson, W[m]. Jackson Cha[s]. Pearsoy, John Davis William Bohanon, Edward Bryan & Jeremiah Bryan with William Kendal their Overseer clear & keep the said road in repair –

28 April 1763[B] (*OCRO*, 83) (Upper Church)
On the Petition of Some of the upper Inhabitants for a Road to be cleared out of the Road near Braxtons old Quarter to come into the Road that goes by the Church Near the Red Oake Level for the Conveniency of Rolling &c Ordered that John Haskey William Lucas, John Cudden & Anthony Foster or any three of them being first Sworn as the Law directs do Veiw the way the said Road is intended to be made & make report to the Court of the Conveniences & inconveniences attending the Same –

28 April 1763[C] (*OCRO*, 83) (Middle Church)
Manoah Singleton as Constable took the Oath appointed to be taken . . . & has for his Precincts all below the Pamunkey road about a Mile below the Church down over Terrys Run to the County line & between the s[d]. line & the road that Passes by Caves Ordinary –

26 November 1763 (*OCRO*, 87) (Middle Church)
Ordered that Richard Woolfolk be Overseer of the road from the Church bridge downwards in the room of Thomas Burrus & that he with the Gang that was under the s[d]. Burrus clear & keep the s[d]. road in repair –

28 September 1764 (*OCRO*, 92) (Middle Church)
The persons appointed to Veiw the Way from Just Below the Church to Thompson foard have Reported that they have Veiwed the Same & find

it a Good Way to Turn out at Nowels path & to go to the s^d. Thompsons foard Therefore it is Ordered that a road be cleared to go the S^d. Way – *See* **25 November 1762.**

25 October 1764 (*OCRO*, 92) (Upper Church or Middle Church or Pine Stake Church)
Joseph Porter appointed Overseer of the Road that Capt. Thomas was overseer on Except that Part leads from the Court house road to the church & that he with The Gang that was under the s^d. Thomas, Except the Hands of the s^d. Thomas & his Brother Edward Thomas's & that he Clear the Same & that Capt. Thomas & his Brother Edward clear the other part

26 September 1765 (*OCRO*, 97) (Middle Church)
A Road to be opened along John Noels Church path and it is Ordered that the following persons do open the Same for one as far as Thompsons foard Viz^t. Jos. Woolfolks 3 hands Thos. Woolfolk 2 hands Saml. Shackleford, John Embre, Thos. Stepp 3 hands John Sutton four hands Thos. Estis W^m. Brown 2 hands, John Brown, John Noel, John Long, Rich^d. Long, W^m. Warren, Sarah Bradbourn –
See **25 November 1762.**

28 November 1765 (*OCRO*, 98–99) (Middle Church)
On the Petition of Thomas Bell to have the road turnd from above Tomohawk to come into the pamunkey road to the Church Ordered that William Bell Thomas Chew Peter Rucker & Saml. Sutton or any Three of Them being first Sworn do veiw the Same and make report of the conveineinces & Inconveinences Attending the Same –

27 October 1768 (*OCRO*, 110) (New [Orange] Church)
On the Motion of William Lucas to have a Veiw for a Road to Turn out of the Main Road about a mile above the new Church and to Come in about a mile Below Ordered That Anthony Foster, Robert Sanford, James Wayte and Jere. White or any three of Them being first Sworn before Some Justice of this County do Veiw the s^d. Way & Make report to the Court of the Conveinences and Inconveinences Attending the Same According to Law –

24 November 1768^A (*OCRO*, 111) (Pine Stake Church)
Grand Jury Presentments . . . the Overseer of The Road from the fork of the Road below the Pine Stake Church to the fork at Wares Old houses for not keeping the Same in Good repair . . .

24 November 1768[B] (*OCRO*, 111) **(Middle [Brick] Church)**
Grand Jury Presentments . . . The Overseer from the fork of the Road below the Brick Church down to Sawyers's Mill run –

27 April 1769 (*OCRO*, 114) **(New [Orange] Church)**
The Way for a Road to go Petitioned for by W^m. Lucas to Turn out of the Main Road about a Mile above the new Church and to come in about a Mile below The Veiwers hav^g. return'd their report and find the s^d. New Way to be a Good and conveinent Way Therefore it is Ordered that the s^d. new way be Established for the road to go he puting the Same in Good repair –

25 May 1769 (*OCRO*, 116) **(Pine Stake Church)**
Grand Jury Presentments We present the . . . Overs^r. of the Road from the fork below the Pine Stake Church to the fork of the Road at Wares Old houses for not keeping them in Good Repair –

27 July 1769 (*OCRO*, 117) **(Middle [Brick] Church)**
John Sutton is Appointed Overseer of the Road from the Widow Bradbourns to Were it Comes into the Church Road and Ordered that he With his hands And the hands of John Browns, W^m. Browns, Little John Brown, John Noells Thos. Ballard Smiths Quarter, Randolph Halebrooks Wm. Gardner, Iasaac Bradbourn, and Reuben Coward and that he With the above Mention Persons do Clear and keep the said Road in Good repair –

23 November 1769 (*OCRO*, 119) **(New [Orange] Church)**
Grand Jury Presentments . . . We also present the Overs^r. of the Road for Not keeping it in Repair that leads round W^m. Lucas's Fence & by the Church –

26 April 1770 (*OCRO*, 120) **(New [Orange] Church)**
On the Motion of John White to have a Veiw for a road from Boxin Camp to the New Church Ordered that W^m. Scott Edwd. Jones, Mathew Davis and John Goodall or any three of them they being first Sworn before Some Majestrate of this County do Veiw the Same and Make report to the Court of the Conveinences & Inconveinences Attending the Same According to Law

27 April 1770 (*OCRO*, 121) **(New [Orange] Church)**
Ordered that W^m. Cox as Overseer of a Road do With the Gang that is Under him open the Old road from the New Road that leads by Brooks's Quarter to the New Church –

28 June 1770 (*OCRO*, 122) **(New [Orange] Church)**
On the Petition of John White for a Road from Boxen Camp into the Road that leads Down to the new Church, The Veiwers have this day made their Report that they find it a Very Good and Conveinent Way if Opened Therefore the said Way When Opened is Ordered to be Established for the Road to go –

27 September 1770 (*OCRO*, 123) **(Pine Stake Church)**
Ordered that Stephen I. K. Smith Joseph Chandler, Henry Wood, and John Kendall they being first Sworn Before Some Majestrate of this County do Veiw the most conveinent way for a Road from the Permunkey Road by W^m. Moor's Gent. to the Pine Stake Church and that they make report to the Court of the Conveinences and Inconveinences attend^g. the Same –

25 October 1770^A (*OCRO*, 123) **(Pine Stake Church)**
Ordered that Alexander Waughs Hands be Taken off the Road from his house to Sear's Old Houses also from the Road from Bryan Sissons to the Pine Stake Church –

25 October 1770^B (*OCRO*, 123) **(Middle [Brick] Church or Pine Stake Church)**
Nicholas Jones Appointed Constable in part of Edm^d. Burrus's Precints from Reuben Daniels to the Mountain Road at the Fork Below the Church and that he be Sworn Before Some Justice of the County –

28 February 1771 (*OCRO*, 124) **(Middle [Brick] Church)**
Ordered that Joseph Bell as Overseer of the Road do Work up with his Gang to the Main Road by the Church and to repair the Bridge –

27 June 1771 (*OCRO*, 127) **(Middle [Brick] Church)**
Ordered That Thomas Bell and & Johnny Scott Gent. do Let the Bridge by the Middle Church According to Law –

29 May 1772^A (*OCRO*, 133) **(Middle [Brick] Church)**
Ordered that the Sheriff pay Zachariah Herndon Nine Hundred pounds of Tobacco by Order of James M^c.Ginnis for part of the Building of the Bridge By the Church

29 May 1772^B (*OCRO*, 133) **(Middle [Brick] Church)**
Ordered that the Sheriff pay And^w. Shepherd Gent. five hundred & Forty pounds of Tob°. by Order of James M^c.Ginnis after Detaining the s^d. M^c.Ginnis's Levys for the Building of a Bridge by the Church

27 October 1774^A (*OCRO*, 145) **(Upper Church)**
Rich^d. Seabrea appointed Overseer of the Road from the Old Church up to the great run Bridge & to have the hands that Work'd under Robert Pearson Except the s^d. Pearsons John Rucker & Jacob Ahart

27 October 1774^B (*OCRO*, 145) **(New [Orange] Church)**
Robert Pearson is appointed Overseer of the Road from Anthony Fosters to the Church road & that he With John Ruckers Jacob Aharts & Tabitha Olivers do Clear and keep the Same in good repair

26 May 1780 (*OCRO*, 162) **(New [Orange] Church)**
The Veiwers have made report of the Road Petition for by W^m. Walker from the Crawfords Ford to Robt. Sanford to leave the Road from the uper End of May Burtons jr Field on the left then Across the great run Between the s^d. Burtons & Jamesons Land from there the Best Way into the Church Path then along the s^d. Path leaving Robt. Pearsons Jacob Ehart & Mordicai Bruce on the Left into the Church Road about a Quarter of a Mile below the Church thence up the s^d. Road the Common Waggon Way into the Road by Robt. Sanfords the s^d. Way is Ordered to be Opened Ordered that Robt. Pearson With the hands that are under him as Ov^r. of a Road also With hands that is in the Precints that Robt. Sanford was Overs^r. of and the hands Under Benj^a. Head W^m. Lucas & Henry White Overs^r. of Roads

22 May 1783 (*OCRO*, 169) **(Pine Stake Church)**
George Bledsoe Appointed Overseer of the Road from Catlett Conwas Gate to the fork of the Roads below the Pine Stake Church and Ordered that Catlett Conways hands & those Below that Worked under Finlasaon Sleat do Clear & keep the Same in good repair

23 December 1784 (*OCRO*, 172) **(New [Orange] Church)**
W^m. Golding Appointed Overs^r. of the Road in the Room of W^m. Bell from Swift run Down to the Ch. Road also the fork of the Road that leads to the Barracks

26 May 1785 (*OCRO*, 173) **(Pine Stake Church)**
Thos. Bohon Appointed Overseer of the Road in the Room of Geo. Bledsoe from Pine Stake Church to Capt Conways Gate

24 September 1787 (*OCRO*, 179) **(New [Orange] Church)**
Ordered that Joseph Chapman be overseer of the Road in the Room of May Burton jr from May Burtons Mill to White Church road

26 October 1790^A (*OCRO*, 187) **(Middle [Brick] Church)**
Reuben Taylor in the Room of Garland Burnley from Berry run to the fork of the Old Chapple road & that he With the gang that was Under the s^d. Burnley with his Own do Clear the s^d. Precints

26 October 1790^B (*OCRO*, 187) **(Middle [Brick] Church)**
George Newman from the Old Chapple Hill by Orange Courthouse & up the fork of the Road by W^m. Suttons & that M^{rs}. Thos. Bells hands be added to his gang

26 October 1790^C (*OCRO*, 188) **(Upper Church)**
James Wood from the fork of the Road by Wilsons Store up to the Old Church With the gang that is Under him do Clear the s^d. Precints

26 October 1790^D (*OCRO*, 188) **(Upper Church)**
Belfield Cave from the Old Church & from Polecat to Eharts ford to Burtons Mill run and that he With the gang that was Under Henry White do Clear the s^d. Precints

This road continues to:

26 October 1790 (*OCRO*, 188)
Joseph Chapman from Burtons Mill run to Boxon camp . . .

26 October 1790 (*OCRO*, 188)
Phillip Seal from Boxing Camp to the foot of Powells Mountain . . .

26 October 1790^E (*OCRO*, 188) **(New [Orange] Church)**
Rich^d. White from the church into the Swift run road & that he with the follow^g. hands towit, W^m. Parrot, George Berry Geo: Shearman Geo: Stephens John White, John Payne Rich^d. White Mons Nicken, Nat Nicken Lemelick Nicken Isaac Cook Geo: Macay Ned Nicken Atrom Nicken W^m. White do clear the s^d. Precincts

26 October 1790^F (*OCRO*, 188) **(New [Orange] Church)**
William Goldon Cont^d. from swift run down to the Church road Also to the forks of the road that Leads to the Baruks

26 October 1790^G (*OCRO*, 188) **(New [Orange] Church)**
William Lucas from the church to R. (?) Paynes school house with the hand return^d. in a List do clear the same

26 October 1790^H (*OCRO*, 189) **(Middle [Brick] Church)**
Ben: Porter cont^d. from Bob. Taylor by Orange Courthouse & from the

fork of the road Below the Courthouse down to Chinch hall

26 October 1790[I] (*OCRO*, 189) **(Middle [Brick] Church)**
Jacob Williams overseer of the road from Williams Path up to the Church with the following hands Joseph Bell Tho[s]. Bowler Miller Bledsoe Julius King James Chiles Rich[d]. Emry John Atkins John Bowling Uriah Garten Thornberry Bowling Malaca Chiles do clear the s[d]. Precints

23 April 1793[A] (*OCRO*, 196) **(Middle [Brick] Church)**
(List of Overseers of Roads) – Oct[r]. 26th 1790 – Jacob Williams – from Williams Path Up to Church run

23 April 1793[B] (*OCRO*, 196) **(Middle [Brick] Church or Pine Stake Church)**
(List of Overseers of Roads) – Oct[r]. 26th 1790 – Absalon Smith – from Woods Mill up to fork road below the Church

23 April 1793[C] (*OCRO*, 197) **(Middle [Brick] Church)**
Appointed – A List of the Overseers of Roads and Precints – Oct[r]. 26th 1790 – Reuben Taylor – from Berrys run up to the fork of the Old Chapell Hill

23 April 1793[D] (*OCRO*, 197) **(Middle [Brick] Church)**
Appointed – A List of the Overseers of Roads and Precints – Oct[r]. 26th 1790 – George Newman – from the Old Chappell Hill by Orange Court house to the fork of the Road near W[m]. Suttons

23 April 1793[E] (*OCRO*, 197) **(Upper Church)**
Appointed – A List of the Overseers of Roads and Precints – Oct[r]. 26th 1790 – James Wood – from Wilsons Store up to the Old Church

23 April 1793[F] (*OCRO*, 197) **(Upper Church)**
Appointed – A List of the Overseers of Roads and Precints – Oct[r]. 26th 1790 – Belfield Cave – from the Old Church up to Burtons Mill run and from Polecat to Eharts ford

23 April 1793[G] (*OCRO*, 198) **(New [Orange] Church)**
Appointed – A List of the Overseers of Roads and Precints – Oct[r]. 26th 1790 – Richard White – from the Church up to Swift run

23 April 1793[H] (*OCRO*, 198) **(New [Orange] Church)**
Appointed – A List of the Overseers of Roads and Precints – Oct[r]. 26th 1790 – William Golding – from Swift run to Church road also the fork

of Road that leads to the Barracks

23 April 1793[I] (*OCRO*, 198) **(New [Orange] Church)**
Appointed – A List of the Overseers of Roads and Precints – Oct[r]. 26th
1790 – William Lucas – from the Church to Payn's School house

23 April 1793[J] (*OCRO*, 198) **(Middle [Brick] Church)**
Appointed – A List of the Overseers of Roads and Precints – Ap[l]. 16th
1791 – Benj[a]. Porter – from Rob[t]. Taylor's by Orange Court house then
from (illegible) Chinch (?) Hall

24 September 1793[A] (*OCRO*, 198) **(Middle [Brick] Church)**
Benj[n]. Porter app[d]. Overseer of the road from the fork of the road by
Rob[t]. Taylor's to the C'House thence from the fork of the road below
the CtHouse to the lane Below Ch Hall that his own hands M[rs] Woods',
Ch[s] Taylor's & M[rs] Thomas's do clear the same

24 September 1793[B] (*OCRO*, 199) **(Middle [Brick] Church)**
George Newman app[d]. Overseer of the road from the fork of the road
above Thomahawk leading by the Court house to the Top of the hill
Above the Church run & that the hands of Baylors where he lives &
W[m]. Tomlinsons & Th[s] Bell & And[w]. Shepherds do clear the Same

27 October 1794(?)[A] (*OCRO*, 201) **(Middle [Brick] Church)**
Grand Jury Presentments We present the Overseers of the road from
the Brick Church to Brockmans Bridge for not keeping Sign Boards . . .

27 October 1794(?)[B] (*OCRO*, 201) **(Middle [Brick] Church)**
Grand Jury Presentments . . . We present the Overseers of the road
from the Brick Church to the Wilderness for not keeping Sign Boards

28 October 1794 (*OCRO*, 202) **(Upper Church)**
Archabald Wilson is Appointed Overseer of the Road from the Old
Church to Blue run And Ehat [*read: that*] the following hands to wit Z.
Burnleys B. Johnson Geo. Newmans Rob & Arch Wilson Abner
Porters, & John Williams's do Clear the Same

24 February 1795 (*OCRO*, 203) **(Middle [Brick] Church)**
On the Petition of William Moore to erect Gates on the Road leading
from M[rs]. Burnley's to the Brick Church it is grant[d]

27 April 1795 (*OCRO*, 203) **(Upper Church)**
Grand Jury Presentments We Present the Overseer of the Road from
the Old Church to Col. Burnley's Shop for not keeping the Same in

Repair within Twelve months last past . . .

28 April 1795 (*OCRO*, 204) **(Middle [Brick] Church)**
On the motion of Zach^y. Herndon for Licence to keep an Ordinary at his building below the Brick Church it is granted whereupon he With Thomas Bell his Security Entered into bond Accord^g to Law

27 February 1797 (*OCRO*, 212) **(New [Orange] Church)**
James Burton appointed overseer of the road in the room of Joseph Chapman Beginning at Burtons Mill from thence to the Church road

26 June 1797 (*OCRO*, 214) **("new Church")**
John White appointed overseer of the road from the new Church to Abraham Howsworths & ordered that the hands that workd under William Lucas S^r. Clear the s^d Precints & keep the same in good repair acc^d to Law

25 September 1797^A (*OCRO*, 216) **(Middle [Brick] Church)**
Jacob Williams appointed overseer of the road from the Brick Church to the place opposite to James Arnolds on Pollocks road and Lewis Brockman from Arnolds to Brocks Bridge and ordered that they divide the hands that formerly worked on said road and keep the same in good repair accord^g to Law

25 September 1797^B (*OCRO*, 217) **(New [Orange] Church)**
On the Pet. of May Burton Junr. for a Veiw of a Road from his house Oppisite to Connollys New Building On the Church Road, Ordered that Benj^a. Head, Robert Pearson, John White and Joel Rucker or any three do Veiw the s^d. Intended Way and Make report to the Court of the Same Accord^g. to Law

22 September 1800 (*OCRO*, 225) **(Upper Church)**
Ordered that Two of the male hands of Robt & Arch^d. Wilson that at present work on the road from the blue run to the old church from this time do work on the road leading from their house to Albemarle

APPENDIX II: THE TOMBSTONE

The eighteenth-century Orange County road orders describe the Tomb-stone, or Crawford's Tombstone, as having been below the (Southwest) Mountain Road and today's Rhoadesville, near the junction of Routes 20 and 650.

The first mention of the Tombstone was in 1729 when the court ordered "the South West Mountain Road Devided into Two Precincts . . . from Craffords Tomb Stone" (6 August 1729 p. 36). After 1747, several orders confirm the identification of this long road as the Mountain Road (Route 20). In 1747, the western half of this road, from the Middle Church to the Tombstone, was divided at Poplar Spring; between 1769 and 1797, the Poplar Spring terminus was called the (upper side of) Berry's run; and from 1795 to 1800, it was called Gum Spring.[1] The head of Berry's Run is below Nasons, and a Gum Spring is noted on a Civil War map near the head of Berry's Run;[2] so Poplar and Gum Springs may have been one of the small waterways which flow into Berry's Run between Nasons and Grassland near Route 20. From 1736 to 1795, other orders describe the eastern half of this road crossing Mine Run. Two Mine Run Bridges are mentioned in over fifty road orders between 1728 and 1798: the lower Mine Run Bridge on the road from the old Courthouse near Raccoon Ford to the Wilderness Bridge and the upper Mine Run Bridge on the Mountain Road (Route 20).[3]

If, as stated in the 6 August 1729 order, this long road from the Southwest Mountain Chapel (later, the Southwest Mountain Church then Middle Church) to Taliaferro's Road (later, the [old] Mountain Road then Alexander Cummins then the [Old] Trap) was divided into two—presumably equal—sections by the Tombstone, then the mid-point between the western and eastern termini of this road should iden-tify the general location of the Tombstone. From 1737, the eastern ter-minus was called Alexander Cummins', and from 1741, it was called the (Old) Trap. In 1736, Alexander Cummins applied for an ordinary license on the head of Russell Run, which is about a mile above the Mountain Road and Locust Grove (16 March 1735/36 p. 15). In 1741, an overseer was assigned to the "road from the Tombstone to the Trapp" and was also ordered to maintain the Mine Run Bridge (23 July 1741 p. 58). The (Old) Trap was near Locust Grove and was a popular location for ordinaries; whether Alexander Cummins' ordinary was at the (Old) Trap or slightly north of it is not known.[4] The Tombstone, half-way between the site of the churches at the road's western terminus and the (Old) Trap at the eastern terminus, would have been someplace near Rhoadesville.

One last order narrows the Tombstone's location. In 1773, a road was ordered cleared from the "Tomb Stone thence along a ridge leaving the Permunkey Mountain," through the land of Adam Lindsay and Thomas Garnett and others to Pollock's Mill, then to the main road leading to Brock's Bridge (23 April and 27 May 1773 p. 137). Later orders describe this road as "Wm. Pollocks Mill to the Mountain road above the Tomb Stone" (26 February 1778 p. 152, 22 October 1778 p. 155). Pamunkey Mountain may have been the 650-foot elevation below Rhoadesville in the area of upper Riga Run. Thomas Garnett and Adam Lindsay lived on Riga Run (*OCDB* 18:168), and Pollock's Mill may have been further south on Riga Run. Brock's (also called Brockman's) Bridge still exists today and spans the North Anna on Route 669 (Marquis Road).[5] This proposed road probably ran from Brock's Bridge on Route 669 to a road equivalent to today's Route 650, which joined Route 20 (Mountain Road) below Rhoadesville and the Tombstone. (Is it a coincidence that a "Mrs. Crawford" is noted on an Orange County Civil War map residing in the area where Crawford's Tombstone stood?)[6]

NOTES

PREFACE

1. William Meade, *Old Churches, Ministers, and Families of Virginia* (Philadelphia, Pa.: J. B. Lippincott, 1857), 2:84–95.

2. Nathaniel Mason Pawlett, *Spotsylvania County Road Orders 1722–1734*, rev. ed. (Charlottesville, Va.: Virginia Highway & Transportation Research Council, April 2004); Ann Brush Miller, *Orange County Road Orders 1734–1749*, rev. ed. (Charlottesville, Va.: Virginia Highway & Transportation Research Council, April 2004); Ann Brush Miller, *Orange County Road Orders 1750–1800*, rev. ed. (Charlottesville, Va.: Virginia Transportation Research Council, April 2004).

3. *Topozone*.com (http://www.topozone.com : accessed 14 July 2007); Ann Miller, *Antebellum Orange: The Pre-Civil War Homes, Public Buildings and Historic Sites of Orange County, Virginia* (Orange, Va.: Moss Publications, 1988); Eugene M. Scheel, *Madison County [Map]* (Washington, D.C.: William and Heintz, 1984).

INTRODUCTION

The Anglican Church in Virginia

1. On 5 November 1728, the Spotsylvania County court fined Darby Queen 100 pounds of tobacco for "absenting himselfe from Divine Service at his Parrish Church or Chappell for two months last past" (Ruth and Sam Sparacio, comps. *Virginia County Court Records: Order Book Abstracts of Spotsylvania County, Virginia 1724–1730 [Part 3]* [McLean, Va.: The Antient Press, 1990], 52).

2. The first mention of a meetinghouse in the Orange County road orders is on 25 August 1774 p. 144. However, it is interesting that the German Chapel (**24 November 1743**), built by the Robinson River Valley German Reformed Protestants, was not called a meetinghouse.

Roads in Colonial Virginia

1. Miller, *Orange 1734*, iii. Historians of greater Orange County have frequently identified colonial roads with contemporary roadways: Ulysses P. Joyner, Jr., *The First Settlers of Orange County, Virginia 1700–1776*, 2nd ed. (Baltimore: Gateway Press, Inc., 2003); J. Randolph

Grymes, Jr., *The Octonia Grant in Orange and Greene Counties* (1977; reprint, Ruckersville, Va.: Seminole Press, 1998); Dewey Lillard, *Land Grants and Surveys of Madison County, Virginia* (Fredericksburg, Va.: Sheridan Books, ca. 2000).

2. Barbara Vines Little, *Orange County, Virginia, Tithables 1734–1782* (Orange, Va.: Dominion Market Research Corp., ca. 1988), 2:213.

3. Eugene M. Scheel, *Culpeper: A Virginia County's History Through 1920* (Orange, Va.: Green Publishers, Inc., 1982), 133.

4. Nathaniel Mason Pawlett, *A Brief History of the Roads of Virginia 1607–1840*, rev. ed. (Charlottesville, Va.: Virginia Highway & Transportation Research Council, November 2003), 6.

St. George's Parish: Grandparent of St. Thomas' Parish, 1721–1731

1. "Germanna History," *Memorial Foundation of the Germanna Colonies in Virginia* (http://www.germanna.org/history.html : accessed 14 July 2007). John Fontaine described the Germanna outpost in his journal entry on 21 November 1715 (ibid., para. 13).

2. Paula S. Felder, *Forgotten Companions: The First Settlers of Spotsylvania County and Fredericksburgh Town (With Notes on Early Land Use)* (Fredericksburg, Va.: Historic Publications of Fredericksburg, ca. 1982), 39. Roads to the Mattapony and Rappahannock Churches are described in a number of Spotsylvania County road orders after 1724.

St. Mark's Parish: Parent of St. Thomas' Parish, 1731–1740

1. William Waller Hening, ed., *The Statutes at Large: Being a Collection of all the Laws of Virginia from the First Session of the Legislature, in the year 1619* (Charlottesville, Va.: University Press of Virginia, 1969), 4:305.

2. Ann L. Miller, "Early German and Anglican Churches of Culpeper County, 1714–1865," in *Early Churches of Culpeper County, Virginia: Colonial and Ante-Bellum Congregations*, ed. Arthur Dickens Thomas, Jr. and Angus McDonald Green (Culpeper, Va.: Culpeper Historical Society, ca. 1987), 6, 11n. 6.

3. Ibid., 11n. 13; Mary Jo Browning, "History of the Little Fork Episcopal Church, 1730–1986," in *Early Churches of Culpeper County, Virginia: Colonial and Ante-Bellum Congregations*, ed. Arthur Dickens Thomas, Jr. and Angus McDonald Green (Culpeper, Va.: Culpeper Historical Society, ca. 1987), 15.

4. **16 December 1735, 17 February 1735/36, 19 October 1736, 23 April 1737, 22 May 1737.**
   5. Miller, *Early Churches*, 9, 12n. 8.
   6. Ibid., 8. This church is called the "New Church," "Fork Church," "Parish Church," "Church in the Fork," "Church in the Great Fork" or, simply, the "Church" in the St. Mark's vestry book and in road orders on **6 September 1732**[A], **8 November 1732, 7 February 1732/33**[A&B], **1 October 1734, 5 November 1734**[B], **16 September 1735**[A], **28 March 1740, 26 May 1743**[B], **29 June 1744, 28 November 1745, 26 July 1746.** Orders for the "road called Bloodworths road near the Church" (**22 July 1742, 24 September 1742, 29 January 1742/43**[B], **27 May 1743**[A]) also probably refer to the Great Fork Church. Another church, Tenent's Church, was ordered built by the St. Mark's vestry on 21 July 1742 (*StMVB*, 32; Miller, *Early Churches*, 9; road orders **28 May 1747**[B], **27 August 1747, 23 March 1748/49**). A chapel in Frederick County, which was formed from Orange County in 1738 but functioned without its own county court until 1743, appears in road orders **27 August 1741, 26 February 1741/42, 28 May 1742, 26 July 1742.**

THE COLONIAL CHURCHES AND CHAPELS OF ST. THOMAS' PARISH

The Germanna Church, ca. 1726–1732

1. Raleigh Travers Green, comp., *Genealogical and Historical Notes on Culpeper County, Virginia. Embracing a Revised and Enlarged Edition of Dr. Philip Slaughter's History of St. Mark's Parish* (1900; reprint, Orange, Va.: Quality Printing, 1989), 4; Joyner, *Settlers*, 176. The Germanna Church might be mentioned on a partially preserved page of 1726 minutes in the St. George's vestry book (*StGVB*, 1).
2. W. W. Scott, *A History of Orange County, Virginia: From its Formation in 1734 (O.S.) to the end of Reconstruction in 1870; compiled mainly from Original Records With a Brief Sketch of the Beginnings of Virginia, a Summary of Local Events to 1907, and a Map* (Richmond, Va.: Everrett Waddey Co., 1907), 88.

The Southwest Mountain Chapel, ca. 1729–1735

1. Felder, 42; Miller, *Early Churches*, 6, 11n. 6. The Southwest Mountain Chapel is usually called the "Mountain Chapel" or, simply, the "Chapel" in the St. Mark's vestry book and the road orders. Between

1734 and 1740, a new "upper Chapel" was also called the "Mountain Chapel," "Chapel at the Mountains" or "Chapel at the Southwest Mountains" in the St. Mark's vestry book (see *The Upper Chapel* and Miller, *Early Churches*, 8–9, 12n. 6).

2. Felder, 42.

3. Joyner, *Settlers*, 88, 181. Concerning Joyner's implied identification of the Southwest Mountain Chapel as the Brick (Middle) Church, see here pp. 35–36.

4. The 1729 St. George's Parish annual accounts record payment of 1000 pounds of tobacco to William Phillips for reading at the Southwest Mountain Chapel. However, in the previous 1728 parish accounts, payments were made only to the readers and sextons of the Germanna, Mattapony and Rappahannock Churches (*StGVB*, 6, 12).

5. Grymes (30, 48, 53–54) located Anthony Head's quarter near Liberty Mills based on Robert Beverley's 12 May 1733 will.

6. Lillard (xii) identified Black Walnut Run as a northern branch of Elk Run. Scheel (*Madison County [Map]*) identified another Black Walnut Run in Madison County flowing into the Rapidan about two miles northeast of Scuffletown; but this run is too close to the Rapidan to make any sense of a ridge between it and the river.

7. Although Robert Beverley worked this land in what was now St. Mark's Parish, he maintained his residence in St. George's Parish where he served on the vestry from 1731 until his death in 1733 (*StGVB*, 19, 34).

8. The **1 August 1732** road order calls the western terminus of this road "Rippons Quarter." Edward Ripping was granted two large patents on the western and southern borders of the Octonia Grant in "Greene" County in 1722 (*VPB* 11:89, 151; Ulysses P. Joyner, Jr., *Orange County Land Patents*, 2nd ed. [Orange, Va.: Orange County Historical Society, 1999], 17, 28, nos. 115, 159).

9. The **6 February 1732/33** order identifies Beverley's Mill as belonging to Robert Beverley. A 1732 appraisal of the Octonia Grant noted that "Beverley had an early mill on Blue Run" (Grymes, 25). Two road orders describing Beverley's Mill: "the Main Road from Fredericksburgh to Beverleys Mill be continued by the Court house" (27 June 1755 p. 39) and "a New bridge over the Blue Run below Beverleys Mill" (28 July 1757 p. 49), place the mill north of a bridge over the Blue Run near the main road (Route 20 or 641)—below today's Liberty Mills—which ran by the Orange Courthouse.

10. Grymes, 13–14, 25, C-11.

11. "Catamount" comes from catamountain, a mountain lion. The Catamount Quarter, or branch, appears four times in the road orders: 6 July

1731 pp. 56–57, **4 June 1734**, 20 July 1736 pp. 16, 17.

12. Joyner, *Patents,* 26, 29, nos. 45, 99.

13. *VPB* 16:434 = Joyner, *Patents,* no. 21; *VPB* 16:433 = Joyner, *Patents,* no. 33; *VPB* 18:540 = Joyner, *Patents,* no. 137; *VPB* 19:711 = Joyner, *Patents,* no. 170; *VPB* 19:999. A 1729 road order describes the Southwest Mountain Road bridging Mine Run, as does Route 20 (7 October 1729 p. 39).

14. Road orders and deeds also describe another Mountain Road and Mountain Run—which still exist—in south-central Orange County.

15. Several Orange County court orders described tithing precincts divided by the "Mountain Road," the "main road" (28 April 1753 pp. 23–24), the "main road to Fredericksburg" (23 May 1751 p. 13) and the "road from the Wilderness Run Bridge" (23 May 1745 p. 107); i.e., Route 20.

16. "Thomas Chews Mill Run" appears in road orders **5 November 1734[A]** and **18 February 1734/35[F]**; "Madisons Mill Run" first appears 23 August 1753 p. 26. A 1759 deed describes land on "part of Pamunkey River [*sic,* North Anna River or Negro Run] known by the name of Chew's or Madison's Mill Run" (*OCDB* 13:26).

17. Fox Point, Fox Point Run, Fox Point Bridge: 1 November 1726 p. 16, 4 July 1727 p. 20, 2 October 1728 p. 29, 2 February 1730/31 p. 50, 1 June 1731 p. 56, 1 February 1731/32 p. 61, 7 November 1732 p. 71, **7 November 1732**, 2 April 1734 p. 85, **5 November 1734[A]**, 25 November 1743 p. 92.

18. An **18 March 1734/35[B]** order for John Lightfoot to oversee the road from the (Southwest) Mountain Chapel Bridge to the Tombstone argues for his residence on this land. The Fox Point land was transferred to John Lightfoot's brother, William, when John died in 1735 (*OCWB* 1:3, road order 17 June 1735 p. 11); William sold the land to Thomas Slaughter on 19 October 1748 (*OCDB* 11:180); and on 25 July 1754, the land was sold to Joseph Herndon (*OCDB* 12:236).

19. Joyner (*Settlers,* 89) said the southern third was deeded to Ambrose Madison, the central third to Thomas Beale and the northern third, with the exception of Lightfoot's 300 acres, to Thomas Hill.

20. Joyner, *Patents,* nos. 10, 11. James Taylor's 1722 patent (*VPB* 11:149) described his southern boundary as "North Side a large Branch of the North fork of the Northanna [Pamunkey River] above the mouth of a small branch." The northern line of Henry Willis' 1728 patent (*VPB* 13:266), which bordered John Baylor's and James Taylor's lines, was described (west to east): "on the South West Side a small branch and on the North East Side a Run Called Bleuing Run and lastly down the Said Run the Several Courses to the Beginning [which started on the]

South Side a run now Called Bleuing Run." This "Bleuing Run" is not the Blue Run in west Orange County and does not appear in the road orders or any other deeds I have examined. Is Bleuing Run today's Tomahawk Run? Does the "small branch" described in both Taylor's and Willis' patents refer to the same waterway or two different branches, and could one be today's Poorhouse Run?

21. Pawlett (*Spotsylvania*, 113) distinguished Crawford's Tombstone and the Tombstone in his index; Miller (*Orange 1734*, 166–67) suggested they may be the same in her index.

22. Several Crawford men appear in the Spotsylvania and Orange County road orders from 1732 after the first appearance of "Crawford's Tombstone" in the road orders in 1729. Scheel (*Madison [Map]*) placed a Crawford's Ford where Elk Run joins the Rapidan; Lillard (xvi) said there was a Crawford's Mountain, Ford and Tombstone where Elk Run joins the Rapidan; and Joyner (*Settlers*, 180–81) suggested that "Though the location of 'the tombstone' remains in doubt, it is probable that . . . [it was on] Route 639." However, the evidence does not support Crawford's Tombstone having been in Madison County or on Route 639, which runs northwest from the Louisa County line near Mountain Run.

23. "Mountain Chapel" and "Chapel" appear as alternate names for the "uper Chapel" in the St. Mark's vestry book between 10 October 1734 and 11 November 1740 when St. Thomas' Parish was formed (*StMVB*, 16, 19, 20, 22, 24, 26, 53–57). The fact that the "uper Chapel" and this "Mountain Chapel," which are associated with William Phillips, are the same is confirmed by the vestry's 10 October 1734 order directing Phillips to read at the "uper Chapel" in 1735 and the 1735 accounts, which credit him for reading at the "Mountain Chapel."

24. David Cave lived east of Monrovia on the west side of the Pamunkey River (Joyner, *Patents*, no. 40) and Samuel Drake lived adjacent to one of Robert Bicker's patents on Berry's Run (*OCDB* 10:75–77; Joyner, *Patents*, nos. 53, 143).

The Southwest Mountain Church, 1735–1744

1. See p. 107n. 11.

2. *StMVB*, 14, 19, 20, 22–24, 53–57; **16 September 1735[B], 22 May 1740, 26 June 1741, 26 May 1743[A], 22 May 1746.** It was mistakenly called the Mountain Chapel two times in the vestry minutes (*StMVB*, 23, 53, 55). Tenent's Church (p. 99n. 6) was also called a "Mountain Church" in a 22 February 1747/48 will (*OCWB* 2:24).

3. Joyner (*Settlers*, 143) suggested the road from Richard Thomas'

Quarter to the Southwest Mountain Church was "likely today's U.S. Route 15 north of the Town of Orange."

4. This long road, which started at Pleasant Run near the Spotsylvania County line, veered south and crossed near the mouth of Terry's Run, then west across the Pamunkey River at Thomas Cook's Ford near Thornhill (*VPB* 13:298 = Joyner, *Patents*, no. 41), then northwest to "three miles from the [Southwest Mountain] Church" and then into the Mountain Road (Route 20) approximates Routes 651 and 612. The original petition for this road, on 25 May 1738 p. 31, described Terry's Run "near Clowders plantation." Jeremiah Clowder's 3000 acre patent was on the mouth of Terry's Run (*VPB* 13:197 = Joyner, *Patents*, no. 62).

5. John Ingram and Thomas Sims leased small plots on Alexander Spotswood's 40,000 acre "Spotsylvania Tract," which stretched along the south side of the Rapidan River from Russell Run to the mouth of the Robinson River (Joyner, *Patents*, no. 43). Since Ingram and Sims worked on roads to the old courthouse at Raccoon Ford (23 March 1736/37 p. 21) and from the mouth of the Robinson through Thomas Sims' land (29 November 1745 p. 115), they must have owned land at the western end of the "Spotsylvania Tract."

The Upper Chapel, 1734–?

1. Rosalie Edith Davis (*StMVB*, 4) said that in December 1733 "a chapel was ordered built near Mr. Mosly Batley's quarter in the Southwest Mountains." Ann Miller (*Early Churches*, 8–9) said the chapel, which the vestry ordered Thomas Jackson to build near Batley's Quarter, "was known as the 'Mountain Chapel,' or sometimes as the 'upper chapel' in the vestry records, it was probably a chapel of ease for those too far away to conveniently attend the new Mountain Church. This little chapel, like the Mountain Church, was within the area which became St. Thomas' parish in 1740." Miller did not suggest a site for this chapel.

2. Scheel, *Madison [Map]*; Lillard, xxvi.

3. Lillard, xxv.

4. On 20 February 1743, Thomas Jackson deeded his son, Thomas, Jr., 100 acres on the "mouth of branch that runs into large branch that runs into Elk Run" adjoining "Thomas Jacksons mill and long branch that runs into Elk Run" (*OCDB* 6/7:89). This description placed Jackson's Mill on one of the many branches of Elk Run, not, as suggested by Lillard (xxiii), on the mouth of Elk Run.

104

5. Almost all colonial Culpeper County court records were destroyed during the Civil War. Ann Brush Miller published the few remaining road orders in *Culpeper County Road Orders 1763–1764*, rev. ed. (Charlottesville, Va.: Virginia Transportation Research Council, May 2004). There is no mention of the Upper Chapel in these orders.

The Formation of St. Thomas' Parish, 1740

1. Miller, *Early Churches*, 6.
2. St. Mark's Parish had 704 tithables when it was formed in 1731 (*StMVB*, 10).
3. J. William Browning, Orange County Clerk from 1919 to 1936, collected the names of thirty-three St. Thomas' vestrymen and a number of Anglican and dissenting ministers from the Orange County order books (William Everett Brockman, *Orange County, Virginia Families* [Minneapolis: The Compiler, 1949–], 3:1, 5–7).
4. Frank S. Walker, Jr., *Remembering: A History of Orange County, Virginia* (Orange, Va.: Orange County Historical Society, 2004), 28.
5. Joyner, *Settlers*, 184–85. In the 18 February 1803 issue of the *Virginia Herald*, Abner Porter advertised the sale of "The Tract of Land, which was formerly the Glebe, in the county of Orange, lying within two miles of the court house, and contains 361 acres" (*Virginia Herald*, 18 February 1803, p. 1, col. 1; Transcriptions of advertisements of land for sale in the *Virginia Herald* published in Fredericksburg, Virginia 1788–1806 [http://departments.umw.edu/hipr/www/fredericksburg/buildads/htm : accessed 14 July 2007]). Rev. Joseph Earnest (Meade, 2:89) said the glebe "after passing through various hands since it ceased to be the property of the Church, is now . . . in possession of . . . Robert B. Marye, Esq." An Orange County Civil War map shows a "Marye" living southeast of Barnett's Ford (Madison Mills) above an unnamed (Glebe) run (Walter Izard, *Map of Orange Co. 186–*, Library of Congress, *American Memory* [http://memory.loc.gov/cgi-bin/query/D?gmd:1:./temp/~ammem_7vjG:: : accessed 14 July 2007]).
6. *StGVB*, 14, 18, 31–32; *StMVB*, 13, 16–18, 27–29. Some of these orders provide very specific instructions for the construction of these glebe buildings.
7. Meade, 2:89.
8. The St. Mark's vestry purchased 215 acres for their parish glebe on 3 May 1731; on 15 July 1731, they ordered the glebe house built; and in 1732, the vestry met at the glebe and paid for the building of the glebe house (*StMVB*, 8, 51).

The Upper Church, ca. 1742–After 1800

1. *VPB* 17:85 = Joyner, *Patents*, no. 139.
2. Scheel, *Culpeper*, 133.
3. "This road has been moved slightly from time to time and has been called by several different names since the county was created in 1734. Generally it has been called the 'Fredericksburg Road' east of Orange and the 'Swift Run Gap Road' west of Orange" (Joyner, *Settlers*, 96). A 28 April 1798 advertisement described a house in Orange County on the "main road leading from Swift Run Gap to Fredericksburg" (*Virginia Herald,* 28 April 1798, p. 1, col. 3).
4. The word "level" described property in several eighteenth-century Orange County documents. On 22 November 1750 p. 10, Richard Sebree was paid for setting up sign posts at "Black oak Levell" but, Sebree's **22 March 1749/50** assignment to oversee the "Road from the upper Church to Heads Ford" suggests this may have been a misnomer for Red Oak Level. The Madison family owned a 733 acre quarter south of the Southwest Mountains called Black Level, (Daniel L. Druckenbrod, "Forest History of James Madison's Montpelier Plantation 1," *Journal of the Torrey Botanical Society* — [July–Sept 2004]; electronic edition, *Look Smart: Find Articles* [http://find articles.com/p/articles/mi_ga4017/is_200407/ai_n9426025 : accessed 14 July 2007], "p." 5). In 1788, the roughly 800 acre Black Level, "about 5 miles above Orange Court-house, on the main road leading thence to Albemarle Court-house . . . lately the property of Major John W. Willis," was advertised for sale in the *Virginia Herald* (16 October 1788, p. 3, col. 3).
5. *Virginia Gazette*, 2 February 1769, p. 2, col. 3; digital image, *Colonial Williamsburg Digital Library* (http://research.history.org/ DigitalLibrary/VirginiaGazette/VGbyYear.cfm : accessed 14 July 2007).
6. Grymes, C1-20.
7. Wilson's Store seems to be described in a 1798 *Virginia Herald* (12 October 1798, p. 3, col. 2) advertisement of the sale of Zachary Burnley's land "on the main road leading to Swift-Run-Gap [Route 20], and adjoining the land of Robert and Arch'd Wilson. This land is exceedingly well to be divided by the road leading from Wilson's blacksmith's shop to the Baptist Meeting house." William H. B. Thomas (*"Faith of Our Fathers! . . ." Religion and the Churches of Colonial Orange County* [Orange, Va.: Green Publishers, Inc., 1974], 13) said Burnley's Plantation is "the present Somerset Plantation." Somerset Plantation was between Liberty Mills and Somerset near Route 231 (Walker, 168).

8. Blue Run Road: **25 November 1743**; Blue Run: **23 November 1744**, overseers replaced on 24 November 1748 p. 138 and 22 November 1750 p. 10, **28 October 1794, 22 September 1800**; Henry Down's: **23 May 1745, 27 September 1745**; Beverley's Mill: **28 May 1752**, overseers replaced on 23 May 1754 p. 29 and 26 April 1770 p. 120 (there is nothing about this road or the overseer assigned to it between 1754 and 1770) and 29 May 1773 p. 138 and 22 February 1781 p. 165; Wilson's Store: **26 October 1790**[C], **23 April 1793**[E].

9. Head's Ford: **22 March 1749/50**, overseers replaced on 27 May 1768 p. 109 and 25 October 1770 p. 123; Great Run Bridge: **27 October 1774**[A], overseers replaced on 26 November 1778 p. 156 and 27 September 1790 p. 186; Burton's Mill Run: **26 October 1790**[D], **23 April 1793**[F].

10. Grymes, 49, 53–54.

11. J. William Browning, *St. Thomas' Parish, Orange County, Virginia*, 1931? in Mary Herring, *Shiflet Family Genealogy Website* (http://www.shifletfamily.org/REF/pointfact.html : accessed 14 July 2007).

12. Brockman, 3:11.

13. Mark Arslan, "Benjamin Head & Martha Sharman (of Orange County, Virginia)" (http://www.arslanmb.org/head/head.html : accessed 14 July 2007), "p." 8.

14. Such mistakes appear other times in the vestry books, road orders and deeds: the "Chappell in the Little Fork" was called the "South West Mountain ffork Chappell" (see p. 8); the confusing variations of Mountain Chapel (see pp. 21–22, 102n. 23); "New Church Road" was probably *a new road to the (Upper) Church* (see p. 32); "Chinch Hall" was probably *Church Hill* (see pp. 37–38); and "uper Church" was the *New (Orange) Church* (see pp. 41–43).

The Middle (Brick) Church, 1744–Early 1800s

1. Ann L. Miller (*Early Churches*, 8, 12n. 3) and William H. B. Thomas (*Religion*, 4) did recognize that the Southwest Mountain Church replaced the nearby Southwest Mountain Chapel, but they placed them in northwest "Orange" County. The Middle Church has been assigned dates "as early as 1738" (Joyner, *Settlers*, 180), before 1740 (J. William Browning; Miller, *Antebellum*, 117), after 1740 (Green, 32) or 1750–1758 (Meade, 2:85; Scott, 43; Thomas, *Religion*, 4).

2. Joyner, *Settlers*, 88.

3. William Meade (1:365) noted that in each parish "There were

always three lay readers, one to each of the churches,—the middle or mother, or Great Church, and the upper and lower."

4. In 1773, the Church in the Little Fork, in St. Mark's Parish, burned down and was rebuilt three years later in brick (Green, 17).

5. Meade, 2:86; Green, 32; Scott, 43; Joyner, *Settlers*, 154.

6. Miller, *Antebellum*, 117.

7. Pamunkey Road near the Middle Church: **22 June 1749, 23 May 1751[C], 25 November 1762, 28 September 1764, 26 September 1765, 28 November 1765, 22 November 1750, 28 April 1763[C]**. The "Main Road" or, simply, the Road below or by the Middle Church is probably the Pamunkey Road: **24 January 1750/51[A], 25 April 1754[B], 25 April 1755[B], 24 November 1768[B], 28 February 1771.**

8. Road orders describing Pamunkey Road: 22 November 1750 p. 9, 24 January 1750/51 p. 10, 28 May 1752 p. 19. Stoney Run was probably today's Berry's Run: in 1739, Thomas Gulley patented land on the branches of "Stoney Bridge Run it being branch of Northanna River" (*VPB* 18:237), and Joyner (*Patents*, no. 52) identified Gulley's patent lying between Berry's Run and Clear Creek (Beaverdam Run). Stoney Run appears a few times in the road orders up to 24 November 1757 p. 52 and Berry's Run first appears 27 July 1769 p. 117.

9. Izard; Walter Isard [*sic*], *Survey of Orange County, Virginia, 1863*, The Library of Congress, *American Memory* (http://memory. loc.gov/cgi-bin/query/D?gmd:16:./temp/~ammem_tblk:: : accessed 14 July 2007).

10. Seven other road orders describe roads, which may have gone to the Middle (Brick) Church or to another church and are so listed in **Appendix I.**

11. The Middle Church is on the Taylor property southeast of Orange Courthouse (Green, 32; Meade, 2:85; Miller, *Antebellum*, 117); "on a hill above Church Run" (Thomas, *Religion*, 5); "on the north side of Route 631 [Brick Church Road], just east of its intersection with Route 612" (Walker, 110); "near the point where Church Run enters Pamunkey Creek . . . near the intersection of routes 612 and 637" (Joyner, *Settlers*, 180—Church Run enters Pamunkey at the intersection of Routes 612 and 631); on a hill where Pamunkey Road crosses Church Run (Scott, 43); where Church Run Road crosses Church Run (J. William Browning).

12. "Bridge over the Church run": **27 February 1752, 23 May 1754**; "bridge over the Run by the said [Middle] Church": **28 March 1755**; "the Bridge below the Middle Church": **23 February 1758**; a bridge or run "below the Middle Church": **25 November 1757, 22 November 1759, 27 November 1761**; "Bridge at the Main Run by the Middle Church": **27 March 1760**; "Bridge by the Middle Church": **27 June 1771,**

29 May 1772[A&B]; "Church bridge": 26 June 1760, 26 November 1763; "Church run": 23 April 1793[A] (see 26 October 1790[I]), 24 September 1793[B].

13. Izard.

14. Hill by the Middle Church: 25 November 1757, 23 February 1758, 22 November 1759, 23 April 1761, 26 October 1790[A], 23 April 1793[D], 24 September 1793[B]. Miller (*Orange 1750*, 282) suggested that "Old Chappel road" (26 October 1790[A]) should read *Old Chapel Hill*.

15. Isard.

16. Scott, 43.

17. "Chinch hall": 26 October 1790[H], 23 April 1793[J], 24 September 1793[A]. It is curious that Barbara Vine Little's (2:185) transcription of the 25 April 1755[B] road order notes a Church Hall but Ann Miller's transcription (*Orange 1750*, 36) does not: "Taverner Beale Gent is Appointed to take the list of Tith[e] in the County from Terrys Run Bridge up the Road to <u>the Church Hall</u> [Miller has only "Church"] on the South side the Main Road up to the Blue Run to the plantation where Francis Wisdom formerly Lived."

18. Two road orders locate Stark's Bridge spanning Pamunkey River on Route 651 less than one mile east of Thornhill: "a New bridge over Pamunky river at the place where Starks bridge stands" (27 October 1757 pp. 51–52) and "a bridge be built over Terrys Run (where the Road from Starks bridge to Fredericksburgh Crosses the said Run)" (28 February 1750/51 p. 11).

The Pine Stake Church, ca. 1746–Early to Mid-1800s

1. Miller (*Antebellum*, 146) and Slaughter (Green, 32) said it was probably built shortly after the formation of St. Thomas' Parish; Joyner (*Settlers*, 182) dated it "probably as early as 1745" and Earnest (Meade, 2:86) and Scott (44) dated it 1750–1758.

2. Because the complete 1740–1746 Orange County order books have not been transcribed, it is not possible to quote this order mentioned by J. William Browning.

3. Meade, 2:86; Miller, *Antebellum*, 146.

4. Miller, *Antebellum*, 146.

5. Joyner, *Settlers*, 184.

6. Izard.

7. Joyner, *Settlers*, 154, 182; Miller, *Antebellum*, 146. Scott (44) and J. William Browning placed it in the same area "about a mile and a half east of Everona," and Browning added that "the spot can be located at

this time by some of the remains of the old church." Slaughter (Green, 32) and Earnest (Meade, 2:86) said it was further north near Raccoon Ford or "near Mountain Run, about fifteen miles northeast of Orange Courthouse, on lands originally taken up by Mr. Francis Taliafero, Sen." And, strangely, Scheel (*Madison County [Map]*) placed the Pine Stake Church in northwest Orange County where the Upper Church stood.

The New (Orange) Church, ca. 1761-1800s

1. This road could not have been near the Upper Church, since the Upper Church is clearly described as being between the Rapidan and Swift Run Road, leaving no room for a "Main Road about a mile above" it.

2. William Lucas worked on roads to the Upper Church **25 November 1743, 27 June 1745, 22 August 1745, 28 May 1752, 22 February 1753, 28 April 1763**[B]. A road "that leads round W^m. Lucas's Fence & by the Church" **(23 November 1769)** was identified by Ann Miller (*Orange 1750*, 293) as a road to the Upper Church probably because of Lucas' past association with roads to that church.

3. Welshman Run probably took its name from William Lucas, a Welshman: "land of William Lucas . . . crossing a branch known by the name of the Welshman" (*OCDB* 18:15).

4. Robert Sanford owned land on Deep Step Run, a branch of Swift Run (*OCDB* 13:274); James Wayte and Jeremiah White had land on Great Run above Ruckersville (*OCDB* 15:104, 112).

5. Charles McLean Andrews, *Guide to the Material for American History to 1783 in the Public Records Office of Great Britain* (Washington, D.C.: Carnegie Institution of Washington, 1912–14) The Library of Virginia, *Virginia Colonial Records Project* (http://lvaimage.lib.va.us/disk18/CR/00797/0001.tiff : accessed 14 July 2007).

6. *Encyclopaedia Britannica*, 11th ed., s.v. "boxing."

7. Joyner, *Settlers*, 177.

8. "Unfortunately we do not know where to locate the 'Boxing Camp'. The intersection of State Road 209 [*sic* 609] and U.S. 33, which existed from early days, might seem a likely site; but currently we don't know" (Donald Covey, *A Greene County History 2002* [Available from the Greene County, Virginia, Historical Society], 29).

9. The road from "swift road down to the Church road" continued "to the forks of the road that Leads to the Baruks." The "Baruks" was very likely the Albemarle Barracks on Ivy Run at Point Fork about six miles

from Charlottesville, which, from around 1778, served chiefly as a prison for British soldiers.

10. *OCDB* 20:38 and "the church road corner to William Lucas" (*OCDB* 19:246, 497, 500) could be the same as the 23 November 1769 road, see also p. 109n. 2.

11. Grymes, 39–54.

12. See p. 106n. 14.

13. The Upper Church is not so called in the road orders after 26 October 1758.

14. Meade 2:84, 94–95. Richard White, a veteran of the Revolutionary War, died 1841 in Greene County ("The Descendants of Edward Watts, 1650–1728," *Tommy Markham's Genealogy & History Home Page* [http://www.tommymarkham.com/Watts/edwardwatts-4.htm : accessed 14 July 2007]).

15. *Ruckersville Baptist Church*, Website (http://ruckersville baptist.org/about.html : accessed 14 July 2007).

THE MINISTERS OF ST. THOMAS' PARISH

1. *StGVB*, 1–11. Rev. Theodosius Staige left England for Virginia in 1725 (Gerald Fothergill, *A List of Emigrant Ministers to America, 1690–1811* [reprint, London: Elliot Stock, 1904; Baltimore: Genealogical Publishing, 1965], 56).

2. Felder (42) dated his departure February 1729, Joyner (*Settlers*, 181) to 1729, Slaughter (Meade, 2:69) to November 1728. Landon C. Bell (*Charles Parish, York County, Virginia, History and Registers* [Richmond, Va.: State Library Board, 1932], 26–29) said he was minister of Charles Parish from 1728 to 1747.

3. William Armstrong Crozier, ed., *Spotsylvania County, 1721–1800; being transcriptions, from the original files at the County Court House, of wills, deeds, administrators' and guardians' bonds, marriage licenses, and list of revolutionary pensioners* (Baltimore: Genealogical Publishing, 1971), F:84; John Frederick Dorman, comp., *Caroline County, Virginia Order Book: 1732–1740* (Washington, D.C.: The Compiler, 1965–67), 429.

4. Green, 6.

5. Concerning Rev. Lawrence DeButts' arrival in Virginia and his appointment to parishes before and after St. George's and St. Mark's Parishes, see Fothergill (24); Meade (2:467); Maryland State Archives, "Proceedings and Acts of the General Assembly, 1762–1763," database, Archives of Maryland Online (http://www.mdarchives.state.md.us/

megafile/msa/speccol/sc2900/sc2900/000001/000058/html/am58-573. html : accessed 14 July 2007), "Lawrence DeButts," vol. 58, p. 573; Linda Reno, "Hannah, Wife of John Attaway Clark," *Rootsweb.com* (http://archiver.rootsweb.com/th/read/MDSTMARY/2001-07/ 0995493933 : accessed 14 July 2007).

6. Meade, 2:76. Rev. Francis Peart is also called "Mr. Pruit" (Meade 2:76, 467) and "Mr. Purit" (Green, 6; *StMVB, 9*), but his name appears as Francis (Frank) Peart in Fothergill (49) and *StGVB*, 21, 34.

7. Andrews (http://lvaimage.lib.va.us/disk18/CR/04753/0002.tiff : accessed 14 July 2007); Meade, 2:124.

8. Joyner, *Settlers,* 177.

9. Ibid., 178.

10. Meade, 2:85.

11. Green, 7, 54.

12. Fothergill, 36.

13. John Blankenbaker (*Germanna History* [Note 679] [http://home pages.rootsweb.com/~george/johnsgermnotes/germhis28.html : accessed 14 July 2007]) called this Mr. MacDaniel, "MacDonald." A report of court cases in the 27 October 1774 issue of the *Virginia Gazette* (27 October 1774, p. 3, col. 1) noted a "James McDonald (or McDaniel)."

14. Joyner, *Settlers,* 154; Thomas, *Religion,* 8.

15. *Virginia Gazette* (1 February 1740, p. 4, col. 2; 4 January 1740, p. 4, col. 1). Rev. Richard Hartswell's paid passage as a minister to Virginia does not appear in Fothergill or Andrews.

16. Meade, 1:442.

17. Joyner, *Settlers,* 135, 154; Scott, 45; Thomas, *Religion,* 8; John Hastings Gwathmey, *Twelve Virginia Counties, Where the Western Migration Began* (Baltimore: Genealogical Publishing Co., 1979), 271.

18. Thomas, *Religion,* 6–7.

19. Andrews (http://lvaimage.lib.va.us/disk18/CR/04751/0001.tiff : accessed 14 July 2007); *OCDB* 9:104–138, 10:338–437, 11:37; road order 25 January 1741/42 p. 63.

20. Meade, 2:88; Green, 32; Scott, 43.

21. Fothergill, 44; Andrews (http://lvaimage.lib.va.us/disk18/CR/ 04858/ 0001.tiff : accessed 14 July 2007); Crozier, F:85.

22. Meade, 2:97; Andrews (http.lvaimage.lib.va.us/disk18/CR/00797/ 0001.tiff : accessed 14 July 2007).

23. Meade, 2:89, 97; Green, 32; Andrews (http://lvaimage.lib.va.us/ disk18/CR/00794/0002.tiff : accessed 14 July 2007).

24. John Rogers Williams, *Philip Vickers Fithian: Journal and Letters, 1767–1774* (Princeton: University Library, 1900), 50.

25. Adaline Marye Robertson, *The Mayres of Virginia 1730–1985*

(Baltimore, Md.: Gateway, 1985), 49–51.

26. Meade, 2:89.

27. Andrews (http://lvaimage.lib.va.us/disk18/CR/00794/0002.tiff : accessed 14 July 2007) and (http://lvaimage.lib.va.us/disk18/CR/00797/0002.tiff : accessed 14 July 2007).

28. Meade, 2:98; "Thomas Martin," *Southern Roots: Martin Family and Friends* (www.tommymartin.net/sroots/scotire.htm : accessed 14 July 2007); *Virginia Gazette* (20 September 1770, p. 3, col. 1).

29. Meade, 2:89–90, 98; Green, 32.

30. *Virginia Gazette* (19 March 1772, p. 3, col. 1 and 26 March 1772, p. 3, col. 3).

31. Rev. John Wingate's transportation to Virginia was paid on 5 October 1771 (Fothergill, 64; *The Foster Family*. Transcribed pages from *Bunch of Barlows* by Elizabeth O. Michaels and John O. Hawkins, 46–50 [http://www.barlowgenealogy.com/BOB/fosterofwilkes.html : accessed 14 July 2007]; Meade, 2:98).

32. *Virginia Gazette* (15 April 1775, p. 1, col. 1).

33. Otto Lohrenz, *The Virginia Clergy and the American Revolution, 1774–1799* (Ann Arbor, Mich.: Dissertation Services, 1997), 88–90.

34. Green, 19.

35. Joyner, *Settlers*, A-39.

36. H. C. Warren, *Bi-Centennial St. Thomas' Parish and Centennial St. Thomas' Church, October 20–21, 1933, Historical Notes* (Gordonsville, Va.: Bibb & Co., 1933), 14.

37. Green, 32.

38. J. William Browning, Slaughter (Green, 32–33), Earnest (Meade, 2:90).

THE HISTORIANS OF COLONIAL ST. THOMAS' PARISH

1. Meade, 1:3–4, 2:74–83.

2. Ibid. 2:84; Warren, 36.

3. Miller, *Antebellum*, 86.

4. Meade, 2:85.

5. This idea that the New (Orange) Church was moved from northwest "Orange" County to outside Ruckersville was repeated—with glaring inaccuracies—by Donald Covey (83): "In 1725 [?] the 'Mountain Chapel' had been built about a mile outside the northeast corner of what is now Greene County. . . . In 1732 [sic] the Bishop of the Diocese of Virginia [sic] sent John Rucker and John Lightfoot to choose a site for the new church. They chose what has been known for years as the

Churchill Farm about half a mile west of Ruckersville for the site of 'The Orange Church'."

6. Philip Slaughter's book was reprinted in 1900 with additional information in Raleigh Travers Green, *Genealogical and Historical Notes on Culpeper County, Virginia.*

7. Green, vi, 6–7, 32, 54.

8. Scott's reference to "(old) Cave's ford" (42) is strange since he seemed to be distinguishing a current and an older Cave's Ford. I found no maps (even Scott's map) showing a Cave's Ford in any location other than on the Rapidan, mid-way between Madison Mills and Liberty Mill, near Route 166. (J. William Browning also used the name "Old Cave's Ford.") Did Scott assume that because both Earnest and Slaughter placed an old house of worship near Robert Brooking's and Benjamin Cave's residence, and that Slaughter located the Southwest Mountain Chapel near Cave's Ford, there was an older Cave's Ford southwest of the known ford?

9. Scott, 42. Charles Peyton Cowherd ("Virginia W.P.A. Historical Inventory Project. Survey Report: The Colonial Churches, 7 April 1936," The Library of Virginia, *LVA Catalogs* [http://lvaimage.lib.va. us/VHI/html.20/0235.html : accessed 14 July 2007]) repeated, almost verbatim, W. W. Scott; the only strange difference was changing Scott's "(old) Cave's Ford" to Cranford or Cowsford.

10. J. William Browning. See here p. 34 for Browning's description of the **23 June 1748** "Upper Church" road order.

11. Thomas, *Religion*, 4.

12. Grymes, 1.

13. Joyner (*Settlers*, 179–80) does not cite a source for William H. B. Thomas. Joyner (*Patents*, 46, Appendix Section 5) also placed the "possible site of the Mountain Chapel" between Liberty Mills and Somerset—several miles east of the Indian Mound and south of Cave's Ford and Montford.

14. Joyner, *Settlers*, 153–54, 179–80, 221, 243.

15. Felder (42) also drew attention to this date in her earlier work.

16. Miller, *Early Churches*, 6, 8–9, 11n. 6, 12nn. 3, 6.

17. Miller, *Antebellum*, 87.

18. See pp. 106n. 1; 107n. 11; 108nn. 1, 7.

APPENDIX II: THE TOMBSTONE

1. Poplar Spring: **22 May 1746, 28 May 1747**, 23 March 1749 p. 145, 23 October 1760 p. 70, 26 March 1767 p. 104; (Upper side of) Berry's Run: 27 July 1769 p. 117, 28 March 1771 p. 125, 26 September

1771 p. 128, 28 September 1780 p. 164, 26 October 1789 p. 184, 26 October 1790 p. 187, 23 April 1793 p. 197, 25 December 1797 p. 217; Gum Spring: 29 September 1795 p. 207, 27 January 1800 p. 224, 22 September 1800 p. 225, 27 October 1800 p. 225.

2. Isard; William H. B. Thomas (*Patriots of the Upcountry: Orange County, Virginia, in the Revolution* [Orange, Va.: Orange County Bicentennial Commission, 1976], 84) mentioned a Gum Spring near Route 20.

3. Two Mine Run Bridges: 26 February 1741/42 p. 65, 23 July 1763 p. 86; Upper Mine Run Bridge: 16 December 1735 p. 14, 21 September 1736 p. 17, 28 November 1747 p. 134, 24 November 1748 p. 138, 23 May 1751 p. 13; Lower Mine Run Bridge: 28 March 1740 p. 44, 24 March 1757 p. 48. The location of the Upper Mine Run Bridge was specified on 25 June 1798 p. 220 when the court ordered the construction of a new Upper Mine Run Bridge "where the road leading from Orange Ct House to Fred[g]. Crosses the same run," in other words, the Mountain Road (Route 20).

4. The (Old) Trap appears on Civil War maps (Isard and Izard). It first appears in the road orders on 23 July 1741 p. 58 and three months later, on 22 October 1741 p. 61, James McCullough was granted a license for an ordinary at "the place commonly called the Trapp." On 23 July 1778 p. 154, 24 August 1780 p. 163 and 26 September 1796 p. 211 the court granted the right to keep ordinaries at the Old Trap. "The Locust Grove vicinity has been known as the 'Old Trap' since the 18th century, and according to local tradition, Robinson's Tavern was built as a replacement for the earlier Trap Tavern, which stood on the old Southwest Mountain Road about a mile to the north" (Miller, *Antebellum*, 157). A 26 October 1790 p. 187 road order describes John Robinson's residence at the Old Trap and he was granted an ordinary license—presumably at the Old Trap—on 25 May 1780 p. 162 and 28 June 1781 p. 166. A "Robertson's [*sic*] Tavern" appears next to the Trap on an 1862 map (*Sketch of a portion of Orange County, north and east of Orange showing the Rapidan River from Rapidan Station to Germanna Mills and the Plank Road to Robertson's Tavern at Trap*, The Library of Congress, *American Memory* (http://memory.loc.gov/cgi-bin/query/D?gmd:6:./temp/~ammem_H4QI:: : accessed 14 July 2007).

5. A 24 February 1757 p. 47 order seems to date the construction of Brock's Bridge to that year.

6. Izard.

115

BIBLIOGRAPHY

Andrews, Charles McLean. *Guide to the Material for American History to 1783 in the Public Records Office of Great Britain*. Washington, D.C.: Carnegie Institution of Washington, 1912–14. The Library of Virginia. *Virginia Colonial Records Project*. http://ajax.lva.lib.va.us/F/?func=file&file_name=find-b-clas27&local_base=CLAS27 : 2007.

Arslan, Mark. "Benjamin Head & Martha Sharman (of Orange County, Virginia)." http://arslanmb.org/head/head.html : 2007.

Bell, Landon C. *Charles Parish, York County, Virginia, History and Registers*. Richmond, Va.: State Library Board, 1932.

Blankenbaker, John. *Germanna History* (Note 679). http://homepages.rootsweb.com/~george/johnsgermnotes/germhs28.html : 2007.

Bontempo, Lydia Sparacio, comp. *Deed Book Abstracts of Spotsylvania County, Virginia, 1728 to 1729*. Springfield, Va.: Antient Press, ca. 2002.

————, comp. *Deed Book Abstracts of Spotsylvania County, Virginia, 1730 to 1731*. Springfield, Va.: Antient Press, ca. 2004.

Brockman, William Everett. *Orange County, Virginia Families*. Minneapolis: The Compiler, 1949–.

Browning, J. William. *St. Thomas' Parish, Orange County, Virginia (1931?)* in Mary Herring. *Shiflet Family Genealogy Website*. http://www.shifletfamily.org/REF/pointfact.html : 2007. (*I could not locate Browning's work in the major depositories of Orange County or Virginia publications.*)

Browning, Mary Jo. "History of the Little Fork Episcopal Church, 1730–1986." In *Early Churches of Culpeper County, Virginia: Colonial and Ante-Bellum Congregations*, edited by Arthur Dickens Thomas, Jr. and Angus McDonald Green. Culpeper, Va.: Culpeper Historical Society, ca. 1987.

Covey, Donald. *A Greene County History 2002*. N.p., n.d. (Available from the Greene County, Virginia Historical Society).

Cowherd, Charles Peyton. "Virginia W.P.A. Historical Inventory Project. Survey Report: The Colonial Churches, 7 April 1936." The Library of Virginia. *LVA Catalogs*. http://lvaimage.lib.va.us/VHI/html.20/0235.html : 2007.

Crozier, William Armstrong, comp. *Spotsylvania County, 1721–1800; Being transcriptions, from the original files at the County Court House, of wills, deeds, administrators' and guardians' bonds, marriage licenses, and list of revolutionary pensioners*. Baltimore: Genealogical Publishing Co., 1971.

Davis, Rosalie Edith, transcr. and ed. *Saint Mark Parish Vestry Book and Levies 1730–1785: Spotsylvania, Orange and Culpeper Counties Virginia.* Manchester, Mo.: (Privately Printed), 1983.

"The Descendants of Edward Watts, 1650–1728." *Tommy Markham's Genealogy & History Home Page.* http://www.tommymarkham.com/Watts/edwardwatts-4.htm : 2007.

Dorman, John Frederick, comp. *Caroline County, Virginia Order Book: 1732–1740.* Washington, D.C.: The Compiler, 1965–67.

———, comp. *Orange County, Virginia: Deed Books 1–8, 1735–1743.* 3 vols. in 1. Washington, D.C.: Dorman, 1961–71.

———, comp. *Orange County, Virginia, Will Books 1–2: 1735–1778.* 2 vols. in 1. Washington D.C.: Dorman, 1958–61.

———, transc. and ed. *Saint George's Parish, Spotsylvania County, Virginia vestry books, 1726–1817.* Fredericksburg, Va.: The Transcriber, 1998.

Druckenbrod, Daniel L. "Forest History of James Madison's Montpelier Plantation 1." *Journal of the Torrey Botanical Society* N.v. (July–Sept. 2004). Electronic edition. *Look Smart:Find Articles.* http://find articles.com/p/articles/mi_ga4017/is_200407/ai_n9426025 : 2007.

Felder, Paula S. *Forgotten Companions: The First Settlers of Spotsylvania County and Fredericksburgh Town (With Notes on Early Land Use).* Fredericksburg, Va.: Historic Publications of Fredericksburg, ca. 1982.

The Foster Family. Transcribed pages from *Bunch of Barlows* by Elizabeth O. Michaels and John O. Hawkins, 46–50. http://www.barlowgenealogy.com/BOB/fosterofwilkes.html : 2007.

Fothergill, Gerald. *A List of Emigrant Ministers to America, 1690–1811.* London: Elliot Stock, 1904. Reprint. Baltimore: Genealogical Publishing, 1965.

"Germanna History." *Memorial Foundation of the Germanna Colonies in Virginia.* http://www.germanna.org/history.html : 2007.

Green, Raleigh Travers, comp., *Genealogical and Historical Notes on Culpeper County, Virginia. Embracing a Revised and Enlarged Edition of Dr. Philip Slaughter's History of St. Mark's Parish.* 1900. Reprint. Orange, Va.: Quality Printing, 1989.

Grymes, J. Randolph, Jr. *The Octonia Grant in Orange and Greene Counties.* 1977. Reprint. Ruckersville, Va.: Seminole Press, 1998.

Gwathmey, John Hastings. *Twelve Virginia Counties, Where the Western Migration Began.* Baltimore: Genealogical Publishing Co., 1979.

Hening, William Waller, ed. *The Statutes at Large: Being a Collection of all the Laws of Virginia from the First Session of the Legislature, in the year 1619.* Charlottesville, Va.: University Press of Virginia, 1969.

Isard [*sic*], Walter. *Survey of Orange County, Virginia, 1863.* Map. The Library of Congress. *American Memory.* http://memory.loc.gov/cgi-bin/query/D?gmd:16:./temp/~ammem_tblk:: : 2007.

Izard, Walter. *Map of Orange Co. 186–.* Map. The Library of Congress. *American Memory.* http://memory.loc.gov/cgi-bin/query/D?gmd:1:./temp/~ammem_7vjG:: : 2007.

Joyner, Ulysses P., Jr. *The First Settlers of Orange County, Virginia 1700–1776.* 2nd ed. Baltimore: Gateway Press, Inc., 2003.

———. *Orange County Land Patents.* 2nd ed. Orange, Va.: Orange County Historical Society, 1999.

Lillard, Dewey. *Land Grants and Surveys of Madison County, Virginia.* Fredericksburg, Va.: Sheridan Books, ca. 2000.

Little, Barbara Vines. *Orange County, Virginia, Tithables 1734–1782.* 2 vols. Orange, Va.: Dominion Market Research Corp., ca. 1988.

Lohrenz, Otto. *The Virginia Clergy and the American Revolution, 1774–1799.* Ann Arbor, Mich.: Dissertation Services, 1997.

Maryland State Archives. "Proceedings and Acts of the General Assemby, 1762–1763." Database. *Archives of Maryland Online.* http://www.mdarchives.state.md.us/megafile/msa/speccol/sc2900/sc2900/000001/000058/html/am58-573.html : 2007.

Meade, William. *Old Churches, Ministers, and Families of Virginia.* Philadelphia, Pa.: J. B. Lippincott, 1857.

Miller, Ann. *Antebellum Orange: The Pre-Civil War Homes, Public Buildings and Historic Sites of Orange County, Virginia.* Orange, Va.: Moss Publications, 1988.

Miller, Ann Brush. *Culpeper County Road Orders 1763–1764.* Rev. ed. Charlottesville, Va.: Virginia Transportation Research Council, May 2004.

———. *Orange County Road Orders 1734–1749.* Rev. ed. Charlottesville, Va.: Virginia Highway & Transportation Research Council, April 2004.

———. *Orange County Road Orders 1750–1800.* Rev. ed. Charlottesville, Va.: Virginia Highway & Transportation Research Council, April 2004.

Miller, Ann L. "Early German and Anglican Churches of Culpeper County, 1714–1865." In *Early Churches of Culpeper County, Virginia: Colonial and Ante-Bellum Congregations*, edited by Arthur Dickens Thomas, Jr. and Angus McDonald Green. Culpeper, Va.: Culpeper Historical Society, ca. 1987.

Pawlett, Nathaniel Mason. *Albemarle County Roads 1725–1816.* Rev. ed. Charlottesville, Va.: Virginia Highway & Transportation Research Council, September 2003.

————. *A Brief History of the Roads of Virginia 1607–1840.* Rev. ed. Charlottesville, Va.: Virginia Highway & Transportation Research Council, November 2003.

————. *Spotsylvania County Road Orders 1722–1734.* Rev. ed. Charlottesville, Va.: Virginia Highway & Transportation Research Council, April 2004.

Reno, Linda. "Hannah, Wife of John Attaway Clark." *RootsWeb.com.* http://archiver.rootsweb.com/th/read/MDSTMARY/2001-07/09 95493933 : 2007.

Robertson, Adaline Marye. *The Mayres of Virginia 1730–1985.* Baltimore: Gateway, 1985.

Ruckersville Baptist Church. Website. http://ruckersvillebaptist.org/about.html : 2007.

Scheel, Eugene M. *Culpeper: A Virginia County's History Through 1920.* Orange, Va.: Green Publishers, Inc., 1982.

————. *Madison County (Map).* Washington, D. C.: William and Heintz, 1984.

Scott, W. W. *A History of Orange County, Virginia: From its Formation in 1734 (O.S.) to the end of Reconstruction in 1870; compiled mainly from Original Records With a Brief Sketch of the Beginnings of Virginia, a Summary of Local Events to 1907, and a Map.* Richmond, Va.: Everrett Waddey Co., 1907.

Sketch of a portion of Orange County, north and east of Orange showing the Rapidan River from Rapidan Station to Germanna Mills and the Plank Road to Robertson's Tavern at Trap. Map. The Library of Congress. *American Memory.* http://memory.loc.gov/cgi-bin/query/D?gmd:6:./temp/~ammem_H4QI:: : 2007.

Slaughter, Philip. *Genealogical and Historical Notes on Culpeper County, Virginia.* (See Raleigh Travers Green).

Sparacio, Ruth and Sam, comps. *Deed Abstracts of Orange County, Virginia, 1743–1779 (Deed Books 9–20).* 5 vols. McLean, Va.: Antient Press, 1985–88.

————, comps. *Virginia County Court Records: Order Book Abstracts of Spotsylvania County, Virginia 1724–1730 (Part III).* McLean, Va.: Antient Press, 1990.

"Thomas Martin." *Southern Roots: Martin Family and Friends.* http://www.tommymartin.net/sroots/scotire.htm : 2007

Thomas, William H. B. *"Faith of Our Fathers! . . ." Religion and the Churches of Colonial Orange County.* Orange, Va.: Green Publishers, Inc., 1974.

————. *Patriots of the Upcountry: Orange County, Virginia, in the Revolution.* Orange, Va.: Orange County Bicentennial Commission, 1976.

Virginia Gazette. 1769–1775. *Colonial Williamsburg Digital Library.*
Digital images. http://research.history.org/DigitalLibrary/Virginia
Gazette/VGbyYear.cfm : 2007.

Virginia Herald. Transcriptions of advertisements of land for sale in the
Virginia Herald published in Fredericksburg, Virginia 1788–1806.
http://departments.umw.edu/hipr/www/fredericksburg/buildads/htm
: 2007.

Virginia, State of. "Virginia Land Office Patents and Grants." Database
and digital images. *Library of Virginia.* http://www.lva.lib.va.us/
whatwehave/land/index.htm : 2007.

Walker, Frank S., Jr. *Remembering: A History of Orange County, Virginia.* Orange, Va.: Orange County Historical Society, 2004.

Warren, H. C. *Bi-Centennial St. Thomas' Parish and Centennial St.
Thomas' Church, October 20–21, 1933, Historical Notes.* Gordonsville, Va.: Bibb & Co., 1933.

Williams, John Rogers. *Philip Vickers Fithian: Journal and Letters,
1767-1774.* Princeton: University Library, 1900.

INDEX

122

www.ingramcontent.com/pod-product-compliance
Lightning Source LLC
Chambersburg PA
CBHW061750270326
41928CB00011B/2453